CORRESPONDENCE INSTRUCTION
IN THE UNITED STATES

THE CARNEGIE SERIES IN AMERICAN EDUCATION

The books in this series have resulted from studies made under grants from the Carnegie Corporation of New York and, occasionally, studies supported by The Carnegie Foundation for the Advancement of Teaching. These books are published by McGraw-Hill in recognition of their importance to the future of American education.

The Corporation, a philanthropic foundation established in 1911 by Andrew Carnegie for the advancement and diffusion of knowledge and understanding, has a continuing interest in the improvement of American education. It financed the studies in this series to provide facts and recommendations which would be useful to all those who make or influence the decisions which shape American educational policies and institutions.

The statements made and views expressed in these books are solely the responsibility of the authors.

Berelson: GRADUATE EDUCATION IN THE UNITED STATES
Chall: LEARNING TO READ: THE GREAT DEBATE
Clark: THE OPEN DOOR COLLEGE: A Case Study
Cleveland, Mangone, and Adams: THE OVERSEAS AMERICANS
Cohen: THE SUPERIOR STUDENT IN AMERICAN HIGHER EDUCATION

OSSIAN MAC KENZIE
The Pennsylvania State University

EDWARD L. CHRISTENSEN
Brigham Young University

PAUL H. RIGBY
The Pennsylvania State University

Sponsored by the

American Council on Education

and the National Commission

on Accrediting

Supported by

The Carnegie Corporation of New York

CORRESPONDENCE INSTRUCTION IN THE UNITED STATES

*A study of what it is,
how it functions,
and what its
potential may be.*

MC GRAW-HILL BOOK COMPANY
New York St. Louis San Francisco Toronto London Sydney

CORRESPONDENCE INSTRUCTION
IN THE UNITED STATES

PREFACE

CORRESPONDENCE instruction is about to mark its centennial year of service in the United States. Yet there has never been the kind of comprehensive study made of this method of instruction that would answer questions of both the correspondence instruction suppliers and the students, the professional educators and the merely curious. Critics have tended to overlook correspondence instruction in their analyses of education in the United States, and literature directed at the problems of correspondence instruction has been frustratingly incomplete.

The Correspondence Education Research Project (CERP)

developed as a response to a recognized need. Correspondence instruction fulfills a significant role in the national educational effort, yet most people, even many professional educators, are ignorant of just what it is and how it functions. CERP attempts to provide the kind of survey that will answer many of the questions that have been raised about correspondence instruction and perhaps raise a few of its own in the minds of those who have not thought much about it until now.

The stimulus for the Correspondence Education Research Project came from the leaders of two of the groups most active in correspondence instruction in the United States today: the National Home Study Council (NHSC) and the Division of Correspondence Study of the National University Extension Association (NUEA). They joined with other enthusiasts to prevail upon the Commission on Academic Affairs of the American Council on Education (ACE) and the National Commission on Accrediting (NCA) to sponsor the survey. The sponsors, in turn, requested the Carnegie Corporation of New York to provide "a grant to finance a study of the past and present status of correspondence education and its future development in the United States."

When the grant had been assured, the sponsors invited Ossian MacKenzie, dean of the College of Business Administration, The Pennsylvania State University, to direct the study. He enlisted the aid of Edward L. Christensen, chairman of Communications and Research, M.B.A. Program, Brigham Young University; and Paul H. Rigby, professor of Business Administration and director, Center for Research, College of Business Administration, The Pennsylvania State University. The study was designated as the Correspondence Education Research Project.

CERP recognized four major gaps that could be filled by a survey of this kind: (1) a history of correspondence instruction, (2) a survey of current problems and practices, (3) an analysis and evaluation of correspondence instruction as a method, and (4) a look at the future. The history and the survey of current practices fill voids in what little reference material is now available. No history had previously attempted to cut across the strong demarcation between private or proprietary suppliers and the university suppliers of correspondence instruction. This study, in contrast, goes beyond this dual distinction to recognize ten different kinds of suppliers and trace the origin and development of each as part of an organic response of the community to meet its educational needs. The survey of current practices serves a different need. It is not meant to be exhaustive; rather it serves as a basis, at a particular point in time, for an analysis of what the method is capable of accomplishing. Information gathered by CERP, primarily for the period 1964 to 1966, gives the reader an idea of what correspondence instruction is achieving now; a CERP analysis attempts to define in what ways this practice falls short of the potential achievements of the method. Finally, CERP takes a look at the future. What role should correspondence instruction play in the education of future generations?

The results of extensive research are broken down and reorganized in this book into the following pattern:

1. Definition of terms and establishment of a context for the study.
2. The origin and development of correspondence instruction in the United States. An attempt to show how correspondence instruction arose as a popular response to a pressing need.

3. Problems facing correspondence instruction suppliers. This section treats problems external to instruction itself but which nevertheless impose restrictions on the quality of that instruction. Such problems include financing, acquiring staff, forming a student body, creating and maintaining a favorable image, and overcoming institutional conflicts.

4. Analysis and evaluation of the method. An examination of the inherent benefits and limitations arising from the nature of the method. A model is presented as a standard for evaluation of how well current suppliers are actually providing instruction for their students.

5. The task for the future. What future problems will face suppliers? What must they do to meet them? CERP concludes the report with a résumé of suggestions (made throughout the text) which attempt to answer some of the questions and serve as stimuli for prompt action by those interested in the welfare of correspondence instruction or of American education in general.

The problems encountered in undertaking a survey of such a mammoth yet diffuse subject as correspondence instruction in the United States are staggering. CERP files are filled to overflowing with interesting data and comments, survey responses, and staff reports. CERP has tried to make this report representative of its findings whenever it cannot be exhaustive or definitive. A description of the methodology used in collecting information for the study is contained in Appendix A. A sincere attempt has been made to eliminate all bias and present only what the survey results warrant. CERP feels that the conclusions indicate definite positions worth discussing and worth acting upon.

The persons most intimately associated with the study are listed in Appendix B. The authors express their gratitude to them in all sincerity. They also thank the many, many others who cooperated so wholeheartedly and were so helpful in furthering the purposes of the study. At every turn the authors found people most willing to assist in any way possible, and for this they are most appreciative.

Ossian MacKenzie
Edward L. Christensen
Paul H. Rigby

CONTENTS

1

Correspondence Instruction Defined

THE Correspondence Education Research Project (CERP) admits to a certain uneasiness in producing a book for both the layman and the professional. Although the former will be familiar with only a general or popular definition of important terms, the latter may have a highly restrictive technical understanding of what each term includes or excludes. To avoid the confusion that might arise from a proliferation of meanings, CERP tries to use specific definitions throughout the text.

The authors feel that the name Correspondence Education Research Project is a misnomer. The term *education* is disturbing because it seems to imply a topic entirely different from that under consideration. *Correspondence education* might be mistaken for education which teaches students correspondence. As a medical education prepares the student for a career as a doctor, a correspondence education might be misconstrued as preparing a student for a career of communicating by letter. Similarly, driver education would teach students to drive, but correspondence education is not concerned with teaching students to correspond.

To avoid confusion, CERP uses exclusively the term *correspondence instruction*. The term *instruction* is intended to strengthen the point that a *method* and not a goal is being described. *Correspondence instruction is a method of instruction in which correspondence is the means of communication between student and teacher.* Much of what the reader may refer to in conversation as correspondence education will be found to fit the definition for correspondence instruction. For those who feel that this distinction is a bit finical or pedantic, CERP can only reply that as the term must be used repeatedly throughout the study, a clear and consistent usage was considered indispensable.

CERP defines instruction, for the purposes of this study, as (1) a conscious, deliberate effort (2) to affect or alter the environment of an individual in such a way (3) as to cause him to behave or be able to perform in some given manner (4) and to do so under specified conditions. This four-point definition covers the intention of the instructor, the means of carrying out instruction, the goal of the instruction, and qualifications or limitations imposed on that goal. A closer look may clarify the main points.

1. A conscious, deliberate effort—Instruction is structured (the two words even share the same Latin root meaning "to build or arrange") in a deliberate manner. Learning from

experience is rarely instruction because it lacks this intentional arrangement.

2. To affect or alter environment—Altering environment is the means used to cause a change in behavior. It can include anything from thrusting a textbook into a student's hands to throwing him into a lake to make him swim. Subjecting him to lectures or class discussions are more familiar examples.

3. Causing him to behave or be able to perform—The goal of instruction always includes some change in the learner. He must be able to perform in some manner for the instruction to be successful. Performance may range from being able to indicate when Columbus discovered America to operating a complex machine. Becoming a better citizen or appreciating art can be the expected behavior as can passing the final exam.

4. And to do so under specified conditions—Even breathing is not always a good thing (underwater, for example). Encouraging a certain kind of behavior must be accompanied by an indication of when that behavior is appropriate. In many cases, learning when not to use a skill is as important as having it. Learning how to replace transistors will only be useful if the student also learns how to determine when they are faulty.

To this definition of instruction, one need only add the qualification that this "deliberate effort" be carried out by means of correspondence to arrive at a suitable definition of correspondence instruction. (Note: Although most correspondence instruction is carried out through the mail, this is only one of several possible means of distribution.)

CERP, however, insists on a further distinction. For the purposes of this study, correspondence instruction refers only to *instruction offered through correspondence which requires interaction between the student and the instructing institution.* Under this definition, a program in which a student receives a book or series of pamphlets but is not required to submit any responses for evaluation by the instructional body would not qualify as correspondence instruction. There is one-way action (on the part of the instructional institution) but not interaction. Programs that would otherwise qualify as correspondence instruction but are rejected because they do not provide for appropriate interaction will be referred to in the text as *self-study programs.* Once again, CERP attaches a strict definition to this term solely for the purpose of clarity in this study. In popular terminology self-study programs, home study, and correspondence instruction may be synonymous.

A precedent for such a strict interpretation was set by Cyril O. Houle in his definition of correspondence instruction in the *Encyclopaedia Britannica.* Houle specifies five components of correspondence instruction:

> (1) specially prepared materials, written in self-explanatory fashion and arranged in a series of lessons; (2) supplementary printed and other materials; (3) a series of exercises to be worked out by the student; (4) the evaluation of these exercises by a competent instructor with the student being informed of the evaluation . . . and (5) a final examination over the whole course.[1]*

It is clear from the above definition that Houle feels student-teacher interaction is essential to correspondence instruction. The supplier who deletes this step functions only as a purveyor of educational materials for home study.

* Superior numbers refer to Notes at the end of each chapter.

Thus student-teacher interaction is identified as necessary to the instructional process. It is worth dwelling on this point for a moment for many of the problems, advantages, and failings of correspondence instruction can be directly related to it. *Feedback* is its technical name, and it takes place in two directions. The instructional institution first supplies the specially prepared materials to the student. The student, in turn, provides (1) feedback for the instructor by turning in worksheets, problems, quizzes, or other kinds of written assignments. These responses allow the teacher to evaluate the student's progress and also to evaluate the effectiveness of the instructional materials used in the first stage of instruction. The instructor reads and evaluates the student responses and provides (2) feedback to the student in the form of written commentary, quiz scores, further study suggestions, encouragement, and the like. Sometimes machines or computers are used instead of instructors, most frequently in cases in which large numbers of lessons must be examined.

One can see how correspondence instruction functions as a method of instruction. But it is important to emphasize once again that it is a *method*. Much confusion stems from the popular misconception that correspondence instruction is somehow different in kind from resident or institutional instruction. This simply is not so. Correspondence instruction shares the same goals and the same educational philosophy as many different methods of instruction. It differs from them primarily in the means, in the method itself. Correspondence instruction and other methods are not mutually exclusive or necessarily inimical. The judicious reader will make an effort to suspend judgment about correspondence instruction until he has had time to evaluate the pros and cons of this method.

In considering other methods of instruction, it is important to clarify a few more terms which may cause some confusion. *Resident instruction* will refer to that instructional method which relies on the student's participation in an institution's resident (intramural) program. This participation in the program of a new environment will demand certain behavior. Lectures, seminars, laboratory sessions, and traditional classes are all familiar components of the resident method of instruction. An *institution* within the context of resident instruction will mean a particular supplier of resident instruction as, for example, Ohio State University, Andover Academy, or P.S. 189. Within the context of correspondence instruction, an institution will be any organization which sets out, perhaps among many activities, to supply correspondence instruction. The University of Wisconsin, the U.S. Air Force, the Moody Bible Institute, and Famous Artists Schools, Inc., qualify as institutions supplying correspondence instruction. *Extension courses* refer to courses offered by a resident institution (as, for example, a university) for students not in residence. The institution "extends" its instructional function beyond its walls. *Continuing education* indicates instruction, not necessarily toward any degree, offered primarily to those who are no longer likely to participate in full-time instructional programs. It is commonly a synonym for *adult education*.

ESTABLISHING A CONTEXT

Correspondence instruction is described in the Preface as performing a significant role in American education. Postponing for the moment the question of whether correspondence instruction makes an important contribution to educational methodology through special qualities, the reader may still wonder just how significant this method is in practical terms. What share of the educational burden in the United States does it carry? Is correspondence instruction a major contributor of instruction today, or is it only a weak sister that reaches an insignificant part of the population?

Estimates vary as to just how many people study by correspondence instruction. A 1962 survey taken by the National Opinion Research Center (NORC) and based on personal interviews of 23,950 adults in nearly twelve thousand different households indicated that approximately 2,000,000 Americans were enrolled in correspondence instruction courses. (Failure to include unmarried students under twenty-one and persons serving in the military may have kept this figure unusually low.)[2] In the same year, the National Home Study Council (NHSC) surveyed correspondence instruction suppliers, receiving 234 usable responses or less than 25 percent of those queried. The NHSC estimate of student enrollment was 3,500,000 or a 75 percent increase over the NORC figure.[3]

CERP made its own enrollment survey for the year 1965, relying on figures given by institutional suppliers of correspondence instruction. CERP concluded that 2,935,000 students were enrolled in correspondence courses for that year (see Table 1–1).

It is interesting to note that the Armed Forces were by far the most prolific group of institutional suppliers in the country. Armed Forces training courses [excluding educational courses offered by the U.S. Armed Forces Institute (USAFI) for the benefit of the military personnel] accounted for 1,767,400 enrollments or approximately 60 percent of all those taking courses through correspondence instruction. Private home study schools enrolled 22.4 percent of the students recorded, while colleges and universities enrolled 8.2 percent.

TABLE 1-1

Estimated correspondence study student body and enrollments by institutional suppliers for 1965

INSTITUTIONAL SUPPLIER	ACTIVE ENROLLMENTS AT ANY ONE TIME	1965 ENROLLMENTS	PERCENT OF ENROLLMENT
Armed Forces	1,301,000	1,767,400	60.2
USAFI	123,900	116,700	4.0
Federal government	23,200	28,200	1.0
Private home study schools	(No estimate)	656,500*	22.4
Universities and colleges	193,600	242,000†	8.2
Religious organizations	47,000	59,000	2.0
Business and industry	38,500	45,300	1.5
Associations	12,300	14,900	0.5
Labor unions	5,000	5,000	0.2
		2,935,000	100.0

* NHSC 1965 estimate (664,155) for accredited and nonaccredited schools less estimated enrollments (7,650) by four association members which are included in association figure.

† Includes National University Extension Association–Association of University Evening Colleges, state governments, and non-NUEA suppliers.

SOURCE: Enrollment figures based upon estimates given by institutional suppliers in response to CERP surveys and interviews. Since CERP's estimate for 1965, enrollments have increased. For example, NHSC reported private home study school enrollments in 1966 of 669,130 compared to 664,155 in 1965; USAFI reported enrollments in 1966 of 131,770 compared to 116,700 in 1965.

The remaining 9 percent of the students were enrolled by the remaining institutional suppliers, who will be discussed in the next chapter.

Three million students constitute a significant part of the total educational enrollment in the United States. When compared with the 5,700,000 students who seek higher learning through resident colleges and universities in this country, this figure seems important indeed. As the overwhelming majority of correspondence students are adults (eighteen or over), perhaps this comparison to other adult students is the most relevant one statistics can make. On the other hand, compared with Sweden where 10 percent of the population of 8 million study by correspondence instruction, we would seem to be making little use of it as an instructional method.

Although statistics may give only a confused picture of the import of correspondence instruction in the United States today, they do help to place the method in a national context. But not until the pros and cons of the method have been examined can the total importance of correspondence instruction be measured. Perhaps it responds to specific needs that other methods cannot meet. The next chapter looks at the needs that first stimulated the development of correspondence instruction and subsequently fed its growth during the century since its origin.

NOTES

1. Cyril O. Houle, "Correspondence Instruction," *Encyclopaedia Britannica*, 14th ed., vol. VI (1965), pp. 544–545.

2. CERP staff paper by Peter H. Rossi and John W. C. Johnstone, 1965. The National Opinion Research Center, supported

by a grant from the Carnegie Corporation, began a study of the educational practices of the American adult in 1962. The central purpose of this investigation was to obtain comprehensive information about the nature and extent of adult learning activities, including participation in correspondence study.

3. "From the Editor's Notebook," *The Home Study Review*, vol. 4 (Spring, 1963), pp. 13–14.

2

Origin and Development of Correspondence Instruction

THE years from 1841 to 1851 witnessed a tremendous westward expansion in the United States. Wherever settlers moved, they took with them a unique approach to education. In a country still expanding faster than it could properly settle its newly acquired territories, innovation became a part of the daily life. Change on the frontier was more a matter of meeting particular problems than of planning carefully for the future. This innovative frontier spirit spread back to the East where it clashed with the conservatism of those who clung to traditional ways.

The unique American educational system took shape during the middle years of the nineteenth century and was nourished by this adventurous spirit of expansion. Education in the United States was marked by its unusual independence from the federal government: "the absence of Federal control, though not of Federal concern."[1] The Constitution did not specify a role for the federal government in education, thereby leaving the responsibility to the states. But the states were slow to accept this responsibility, and early in the nineteenth century much of the educational burden still rested on religious or private institutions.

The principle of equality of educational opportunity was well established by the time of the Civil War, but it was not equality as we would recognize it today. It had been only a short time since women were first admitted to public education, and there were still very few colleges or universities that accepted them. Noncitizens, Negroes, and the very poor often found their educational opportunities far from equal to those of the son of the Boston banker. In fact, they may often have been denied an education altogether.

By 1870, however, the principle of free public elementary education was generally in practice throughout the country. The states had recognized a responsibility to collect taxes to support a school system whose doors would be open to all residents. The high school, nevertheless, was still a controversial concept. Not until 1874, when the Michigan Supreme Court ruled that the city of Kalamazoo was legally entitled to finance its high school program with municipal funds, did the tax-supported high school receive the unqualified endorsement it needed for survival.

Colleges and universities had generally thrown off their sectarian shackles, but most of them remained private. A few states had entered the supplier market but as competitors with private institutions, not as their replacements. Oberlin had been the first college to admit women on an equal footing with men. When it began operation in 1833, four women entered as the country's first female candidates for recognized college degrees. By 1870, several other institutions of higher learning had become coeducational.

As the century progressed, industrialization took a firm hold in the United States. The Industrial Revolution, sparked in England, found its most virile advocate in the United States. Railroads spanned the nation, factories crowded its valleys in the East and North, and capitalism became its way of life. The public education system began to recognize a need to train the vast body of workers needed to run an industrial nation. The demands were prodigious. At the turn of the century, some 90 percent of the working population had not graduated from high school.[2] Part of the reason was the failure of the high schools to adapt themselves to the demands of an industrialized society. Though as late as 1920 fewer than one student in five who entered high school went on to college, a college preparatory course was prescribed for the vast majority of all high school students. According to John S. Noffsinger, one of the early experts on correspondence instruction: "It was in the spirit of revolt against this rank injustice . . . that supervised correspondence study was born in the United States."[3]

THE COUNTRY'S INSTRUCTIONAL NEEDS: 1870

The expansion westward, the Industrial Revolution, and the increasing role of the woman in American society were exerting considerable pressure on the American educational system in 1870. New needs for both general education and technical training added to the strain that a rapidly increasing population was placing on conventional suppliers of instruction.

Correspondence instruction was one of the resourceful responses which arose to meet this need. Three different kinds of demands on the country's instructional resources were important stimuli to the rise of correspondence instruction: (1) educational, (2) training, and (3) general. These three categories, which apply to all types of instruction, will be particularly useful in understanding the origin and development of .correspondence instruction later in this chapter.

Educational

By *education* CERP means the general development and cultivation of the mental and moral faculties of the individual. In a democracy, this education provides the basis for sound government by creating good citizens who are fit and prepared to take part in running their country. Education also provides a background for vocational development, but it does not set out to give each individual specific job training. The product of a good education is a literate individual, aware of the problems of his society and prepared to attempt to deal with them.

Training

CERP defines *training* as a much more specific function than education. Training aims to prepare the trainee for a specific skill or task. Technical proficiency is the basis for efficient operation. In a competitive economy, this proficiency is the key to production and profit. The highly trained individual knows his skill and excels in its performance. Even with no formal education, he may perform an important service to society through his skill. Training is, above all, a pragmatic function:

> [Education] in industry should be judged only by what it sets out to be. . . . It is not concerned with the worker's background or with his advancement in any aspect not related to his efficiency as a worker. It does not aim to teach him anything not connected with his work or useful in his work, in the last analysis with anything not conducive to greater efficiency and therefore greater return to his employer. To be sure, greater efficiency will also advance the worker in rank and pay, but that is not industry's motive. In other words, the only test which industry applies is, does it pay?[4]

General

There are some needs that do not correspond to the educational function or to training as defined above. Individuals may seek instruction to satisfy their curiosity, to learn some skill for recreational purposes, or to be able to accomplish a single task without necessarily becoming proficient in the complex skill ordinarily associated with it. For example, a farmer might want to know how to mend a particular machine without qualifying as a skilled mechanic, or a businessman might want to learn to paint for no other motive than his own satisfaction. All these needs CERP lumps together as general demands on the educational system.

THE INDIVIDUAL'S INSTRUCTIONAL NEEDS

The principle of democracy demands a democratic approach to education. In the United States, a policy proposing the equality of educational opportunity for all was developed to meet this demand. To Knute O. Broady, speaking at the First International Conference on Correspondence Education in 1938, this principle continues to define the central goal of the democratic system of education, "By equality of educational opportunity we mean extending education to everyone, no matter how humble his birth, no matter where he may live, and no matter what his reasonable aspirations may be."[5]

But an educational philosophy founded on this principle is necessarily going to create some pretty stiff problems. Can the state fulfill its responsibility merely by setting up a resident system and allowing all who apply to participate? Or must it also go out of its way to ensure that the individual takes advantage of what is offered him? Compulsory attendance laws indicate that the states recognize a need to go beyond the role of disinterested supplier.

What about those who, for one reason or another, cannot participate in the established system? Are they not still entitled to an education equal to that offered everyone else? Yet to establish a different kind of resident institution to serve every problem would overstrain any state's financial resources. Before examining how the country first met the challenge of educating these people, CERP takes a look at their special problems within the context of the three different categories of instructional needs.

Education

One of the major obstacles to participation in conventional educational programs is geographical separation. In many rural communities, assembling students at a central school still presents a difficult problem today. How much worse a problem confronted the pioneer family living on the Great Plains or the frontier farmer living far from any school! This difficulty is compounded by the farmer's need for manual labor; as a result, he is unwilling to send his children too far from the farm for any length of time. If these students cannot be brought to the schools, can instruction be sent to them?

> One of the first uses of correspondence within a public school system was in the province of Victoria, Australia, in 1914, when wives of some forest rangers living in a remote mountain section asked for assistance in the education of their children. The state department mailed them texts and suggested assignments.[6]

And the Division of Supervised Study of North Dakota State University still lists as a prime objective: "to make high school available to all farm boys and girls."[7]

In spite of compulsory attendance laws, there is always some part of the adult population which has not received the education its problems demand. Especially significant during the last quarter of the nineteenth century and early years of the twentieth was an influx of immigrants. Many of these had received only a marginal education in their own country; nearly all needed reeducation if they were to become good citizens of the United States.

Some individuals or groups are unable to participate in educational programs because their occupations conflict with conventional requirements for resident study. Military personnel cannot take time off from military training or duties to attend resident classes. Housewives cannot leave children alone or perhaps find that their husbands' occupations take them far from resident centers of learning. Farm workers and children are tied to a calendar that often conflicts with resident instruction. Workers in business or industry, many of whom may have cut short their education to go out and earn a living, work during the hours normally allocated to classes. Such conflicting demands usually result in work taking priority and study being neglected.

The physically handicapped child has a transportation problem that is often as serious as that of the geographically isolated child. The handicapped child suffers further in that he may not be able to participate in some parts of the program even if he gets to a typical resident school. The dropout or flunk-out who wishes to participate in some type of instructional program may be refused because of his past record or perhaps may find himself psychologically unable to reenter a system which has branded him a failure.

Another obstacle to education concerns religious instruction. Ever since Article I of the Constitution was interpreted as ruling out religious study in public schools, public school-children have had to look elsewhere for religious or Bible instruction. Sunday school or evening classes have been established by the various religious institutions, but the same problems that keep students from attending public classes frequently keep them from these religious schools. It should be added that some religious groups seek converts through proselyting or persuasive education. These groups are deeply concerned with making religious education available to everyone.

The enrichment of substandard school curricula aims to correct a problem affecting the student attending a resident institution. Small schools or schools in particularly poor areas are frequently incapable of meeting many students' needs. Both advanced and remedial courses tend to be left out of limited curricula. Teaching foreign languages and laboratory sciences is often beyond the capabilities of teachers or the physical plant in poor schools. But even many affluent school systems cannot or choose not to supply specialized courses when the demand is small, often too small to fill a conventional class. Vocational courses are often lacking from school curricula because teaching them would involve too great an expenditure of school board funds and faculty energies. Overflow classes and limited facilities are problems that face nearly every school at some time.

These problems affect the individual's right to equal educational opportunity as profoundly as personal obstacles. Broady, who helped pioneer the University of Nebraska program to enrich high school curricula through correspondence instruction, summarized that program's goals in a CERP staff paper:

> The purpose was to enable these schools, whatever their size, to offer through correspondence study any course, academic or vocational, which for any reason—limited demand, lack of qualified faculty, schedule conflicts or absence from school for physical reasons or because of inaccessibility—was not available by means of regular classroom instruction.

Whatever the obstacle preventing an individual from obtaining a decent education, educators have felt the need to overcome it.

Training

Although obstacles of the kind mentioned above received prompt attention from educators, a large portion of the country's instructional needs were ignored for many years. CERP has already quoted Noffsinger on the unjust assumption that a college preparatory course is the best program for all students. Although it took a long time for the idea to gain acceptance, educators gradually came to interpret "equal opportunity" to mean providing vocational training for those who seek it.

The rapid industrialization of the country created demands that the public school system was not prepared to meet. Previously, manual labor had been able to satisfy the demand for manufactured goods; now skilled workers were needed to run complex machinery. Producing and repairing this machinery became a major industry. The continued advancement of technology and constant invention of new means of production meant that a skilled worker could no longer be complacent in his job. He had to face the prospect of nearly continuous retraining to keep up with industrial change. In the professions, since new techniques and equipment required increasingly skilled practitioners, requirements were raised for obtaining a license or certification.

Demands for more sophisticated skills were created by the changeover to a technological military. The days of the militia, when each man fended for himself, passed into an era of highly technical operation in which every foot soldier was supported by a complex network of technical experts who kept him trained, fed, mobile, supplied with advanced weapons, and in constant communication with the rest of his forces.

Federal government functions grew both in scope and in complexity. Collecting taxes, delivering the mail, drafting soldiers, and regulating air traffic, to mention just a few functions, became mechanized and required trained personnel to administer their efficient operation.

General

Individuals with general instructional requirements are often trying to fill gaps in their general education or their vocational training. Sometimes their needs are vital to their ability to function in society; more often their needs indicate optional goals they choose to set for themselves.

A student may wish to take one or a limited number of courses of the educational type, not in order to complete his education but merely to satisfy an interest in the subjects. For many reasons—lack of prerequisite qualifications, refusal to take full-time instruction, restrictions on class enrollments —he may be denied the opportunity to take them at a resident institution. For those enrolled in a resident educational program, attempts to gain a limited amount of vocational training may be frustrated by institutional inflexibility. For those not associated with some company or organization (professional, labor, trade, etc.), certain kinds of vocational training may actually be unavailable at any price.

Among those seeking general instruction are persons already trained for their vocation who require additional training to keep up with new developments. They may need to acquire this instruction without taking time off from work, thus being denied an opportunity to attend regular classes. There are also some adults who hold a job but find they need additional instruction for advancement. Furthermore, some workers find that they need to learn about some topic not covered in their past instruction but cannot attend resident classes.

However, the majority of seekers after general instruction seem to be avocationalists. As technological advancement provides for more leisure time, and as an increasingly affluent society has more dollars to spend on recreation, hobbies and other spare-time activities increase greatly. The hobbyist may want to learn how to skin dive, how to redecorate his living room, when to plant flowers, or how to cook. The established educational system has never felt such interests of the external student to be within its instructional province.

MOTIVE OF THE INSTRUCTIONAL SUPPLIER

In most cases, the motive of the supplier is closely related to the goal of the kind of instruction. Educational suppliers are primarily intent on producing the special entity known as the well-rounded individual. They believe they are performing a service, not merely a set task. They often feel strongly about the right of the student to a good education, and they tend to consider it their duty to serve their country's educational needs. They generally consider education beyond the realm of profit, although they defend the right of the private institution to coexist with tax-supported schools and universities. *Colleges and universities, state and local governments, religious and philanthropic institutions, and the U.S. Armed Forces Institute (USAFI) are the major suppliers of correspondence instruction for educational purposes.*

Suppliers of instruction for their own training purposes have a well-defined primary goal. They want to improve the operation of an organization and seek to accomplish this by training its members. Technical skill yields efficient operation, which in turn leads to higher profits. Increased training also improves service, leading to satisfied customers and a more profitable business. The improved efficiency which leads to increased output is generally the motivation behind the training—at least from the suppliers' point of view. *Major sup-pliers of training instruction through correspondence are the Armed Forces, business and industry, professional and trade organizations, the federal government, and labor unions.*

Suppliers of general instruction are difficult to character-ize. They offer nearly every kind of course obtainable from the other two groups of suppliers and many other courses that only they supply. The vast majority of the general sup-pliers are in the business for one main reason, typified by one proprietor's candid response to a CERP question about his school's objectives, "to make a profit for the owner." They have a service to sell, and they operate much as any other commercial venture. They may be idealists or scoundrels, but for the most part they share a desire—while providing a service —to produce an increase of income over expenditure. *These suppliers are known as the private home study schools.*

MEETING A DEMAND:

THE RISE OF CORRESPONDENCE INSTRUCTION

Correspondence instruction owes much to the frontier spirit which encouraged a flexible approach to instructional prob-lems. The typically American pragmatic approach, insisting that there is always some way to overcome every obstacle, de-veloped correspondence instruction to serve those whose needs were not being met by the existing resident system.

European Influence

Yet the basic concept and pattern of correspondence instruc-tion were European developments. As early as 1850, English educators were considering the possibilities for extending the university beyond its walls to meet the needs of nonresidents. In that year William Sewell, fellow and senior tutor of Exeter College, is quoted as saying, "Though it may be impossible to bring the masses requiring education to the university may it not be possible to carry the university to them?"[8]

As the English extension system grew, its influence spread. The concept of extramural instruction eventually spawned several kinds of instructional methods, all aimed at bringing education to those unable to attend resident institutions. Walton S. Bittner and Hervey F. Mallory, whose *University Teaching by Mail* is one of the sources of historical information about correspondence instruction, considered the "ideal of extending opportunity . . . in the English university extension movement . . . to be the ancestor of correspondence teaching."[9]

On the Continent, the offering of courses through the mail was an established practice by 1856. Charles Toussaint, a French teacher, and Gustav Langenscheidt, a German writer, opened a school for teaching language by correspondence. The Toussaint-Langenscheidt Correspondence School remained in operation for over eighty years, finally closing during World War II.

AMERICAN EDUCATORS REACT
TO THE NATION'S SPECIAL NEEDS

Anna Eliot Ticknor

The daughter of a Harvard professor[10] founded the first correspondence instruction program in the United States. After inquiring about similar organizations in England, Anna Eliot Ticknor founded the Society to Encourage Studies at Home. The Boston-based operation, begun in June of 1873, functioned continuously for twenty-four years before its founder's death in 1897 put an end to its activities.

Anna Ticknor looked upon her society as performing a humanitarian function. It carried learning to a following that reached a peak of 1,000 in 1882. Many of her students were women, for despite the progress made in providing equal educational opportunities for them, conservatism and individual prejudice still kept many women safely tucked away by the hearth.

The idea of an interchange of letters between student and teacher appears to have originated with Anna Ticknor. Monthly correspondence with guided readings and frequent tests formed an essential part of the society's personalized instruction. Six different departments—history, science, art, literature, French, and German—offered a total of twenty-four subjects. Although enrollment declined seriously in the society's final years of operation, this slackening off is apparently attributable more to the founder's insistence upon "working quietly" and avoiding all promotion or advertising than to dissatisfaction with the quality of instruction.

Illinois Wesleyan

Anna Ticknor's school was a private institution, although it might well be called public-spirited. The second institution to offer correspondence instruction was an established university. Illinois Wesleyan University, a denominational institution, was established in Bloomington and endowed by members of the

Methodist Church in 1850. It received a charter with degree-granting authority from the state of Illinois in 1853. In 1873, the same year Anna Ticknor's society began operation, Illinois Wesleyan began offering nonresident courses to prepare students for university examinations. Correspondence work could lead to A.B. or Ph.B. degrees or eventually to an A.M. or a Ph.D.

The Illinois Wesleyan program apparently failed to convince its critics that equivalent standards were being maintained for resident and correspondence students. Some institutions of higher learning refused to recognize a degree granted wholly on study done by correspondence. In 1906, the University Senate of the Methodist Institutions decreed that all colleges in the federation had four years in which to phase out their correspondence programs.

The Correspondence University

Many educators recognized a more broadly based need for nonresident educational services than could be met by the two programs mentioned above. They felt that techniques developed for these programs would be "equally serviceable in severer study."[11] Thirty-two professors from different colleges, "from Harvard University in the East to the Johns Hopkins University at the South and the University of Wisconsin at the West,"[12] united with this idea in mind in 1883 to form the Correspondence University with its base of operations in Ithaca, New York.

Despite its name, the Correspondence University had neither a state charter nor the authority to grant degrees. It was a university only in respect to the ambitions of its curriculum. It was designed, however, to supplement the teaching of resident institutions, not to rival or replace them.

The Father of Correspondence Instruction

Although Anna Ticknor is credited with being the founder of correspondence instruction in the United States, the person most responsible for the acceptance of the method was William Rainey Harper. As a young teacher at Baptist Theological Seminary in Morgan Park, Illinois, Harper was disturbed by the inability of some students to take his courses because of limited facilities at the seminary. There was such a demand for Harper's courses in Hebrew that he succeeded in obtaining permission from the seminary to offer additional courses during the summer recess. Yet some students were unable to attend the summer classes either, and Harper's concern for them led to the idea of preparing correspondence courses. His good friend, Thomas W. Goodspeed, described Harper's reaction to being unable to meet all his students' demands in the classroom:

> He conceived the idea of teaching Hebrew by correspondence, . . . The first lesson was sent out February 14, 1881. As his friend and fellow-professor, Dean E. B. Hulbert, afterward said, the response was so encouraging that "the next year the lesson slips were printed . . . and alluring circulars were sent broadcast over the land, inviting the study or re-study of the language of the Old Testament. . . . The renaissance had come indeed."[13]

As Harper's prestige and reputation began to grow, his services were sought by other institutions interested in his correspondence experiments. The chancellor of the Chautauqua University, John H. Vincent, succeeded in bringing the young Harper to the summer assembly as a teacher of Hebrew. In 1885, after having organized its school of languages, he was made principal of the Chautauqua College of Liberal Arts.[14] *The Chautauqua Movement* (1886) quotes Harper at length on the correspondence system, giving an excellent analysis of the procedures, accomplishments, and drawbacks of correspondence instruction during its early years in the United States.[15]

The growth of Harper's Correspondence School of Hebrew was remarkable. In 1884 it was placed under the management of the American Institute of Hebrew with about seventy professors of Hebrew and Old Testament subjects as teachers. "In 1886, when Harper moved to Yale Divinity School as a professor of Semitic Languages, the Correspondence School went to New Haven with him."[16] A few years later it became the American Institute of Sacred Literature.

University of Chicago

After five scholarly and productive years at Yale, Harper resigned to become president of the new University of Chicago. When Chicago opened in 1892, it was organized into five divisions, bearing a marked similarity to the organizational pattern at Chautauqua. Three of the divisions introduced new features into university organization. One of the three, University Extension, included provisions for correspondence instruction. This was in keeping with President Harper's goal, a revolutionary concept in American education at the time: "the keynote of the University of Chicago was *service*; service, not restricted to the students in its classrooms, but extended to all classes."[17] The home study department of the University of Chicago continued to provide this service for seventy-two years until it closed in 1964.

Other Universities Follow Chicago's Lead

Chicago's home study department met with serious academic opposition both within and without the university. Yet several other universities picked up the idea; by the outbreak of World War I, more than a dozen colleges and universities were offering some form of correspondence instruction.

Pennsylvania State College responded primarily to a need for greater training in agricultural and domestic sciences. It offered thirty courses in these disciplines free of charge, providing a needed service to Pennsylvania farmers. Baylor University in Waco, Texas, opened a correspondence program in 1897 at about the same time as the state normal school at Willimantic, Connecticut, began a correspondence operation.

But the first university to follow Chicago and establish a correspondence teaching department along institutional lines was the University of Wisconsin. President Van Hise, when opening the correspondence instruction department in 1906, declared that "responsibility for the dissemination of accumulated knowledge in assimilable form for all people was an equal function of the modern university, with that of resident teaching and research."[18] Wisconsin's program was largely a response to the demands on universities to broaden their curricula and adapt their teaching to the needs of the population for vocational training. Van Hise, speaking at the first National University Extension Conference at Madison, Wisconsin, in 1915, explained,

> The Chicago correspondence work includes that required for entrance to the university and courses of college grade . . .

At Wisconsin the correspondence work differs from that in Chicago in that a large proportion of it is vocational.[19]

Hard on the heels of Wisconsin, seven other universities founded correspondence programs between 1906 and 1910. The University of California at Berkeley started a correspondence department in 1913. The University of Nebraska sponsored a program that, along with the program of Wisconsin, has been a pioneer experiment in employing new applications of correspondence instruction to educational problems.

By 1964, Berkeley was running the country's largest university-operated correspondence instruction program with Nebraska second in student enrollment. Sixty-four different universities reported operating correspondence instruction programs. Most of these programs offered courses for degree

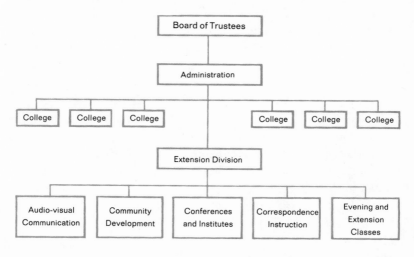

Figure 2–1 Typical organization of a university extension service. (Source: Correspondence Education Research Project, 1967.)

credit, and a large number were engaged in supplying high school courses. Nearly half the universities reported offering noncredit courses, and considerably fewer prepared courses for certification credit. The typical position of a correspondence division within the university organizational structure is shown in Figure 2–1. A conservative estimate puts the total number of university-supplied correspondence courses at nine thousand.

Meeting the Need for High School Courses

With the enactment in many states of compulsory school attendance laws about 1890, educators focused their attention on the high school. Preventing dropouts became a major concern of the American educational system. Many suppliers of correspondence instruction felt they had a duty to offer a second chance to these dropouts, perhaps by providing vocational training for credit while the high school was still slow to accept nonacademic courses. The concept of a "high school equivalency" education began to grow in stature.

The leading innovator in high school courses by correspondence was Sidney B. Mitchell, superintendent of schools in Benton Harbor, Michigan. He first began using correspondence instruction in 1923 to fill the vocational needs of terminal students who were still attending high school. Mitchell did not create his own instructional material but contracted for courses from cooperating correspondence schools which he then offered to an experimental group of ten students. He first approached the American School and later the International Correspondence Schools to supply these courses. As a result, Benton Harbor students were able to choose from over four hundred vocational subjects.[20] The Benton Harbor plan, which

Mitchell dubbed "supervised correspondence instruction," was controversial from the outset. The plan called for supervision of the students by a teacher interested in guidance, during released time from class. Through this supervision, the correspondence instruction could be integrated into the high school's regular instructional program. The Benton Harbor program, still operating satisfactorily in 1965, proved both economical and practical and soon spread to other high schools.[21] Noffsinger reported: "During the seven-year period following the inauguration of the supervised correspondence method at Benton Harbor, similar experiments were started at more than one hundred public high schools."[22]

The University of Nebraska, with financial assistance from the Carnegie Corporation, was the first state university to experiment with supervised correspondence instruction in the high school. In 1929 Nebraska pioneered a program in which high schools provided supervision for courses taken by correspondence, usually during the regular school day. In the 1930s university interest in enriching high school programs resulted in the proliferation of supervised correspondence instruction. Of the sixty-four universities which were members of the National University Extension Association (NUEA) in 1965, forty-two were offering courses by correspondence at the high school level.

For the most part, universities became leaders in high school correspondence instruction because neither the states nor the local school systems seemed capable of accepting the task. The Phoenix Union High School appears to have been the lone exception. It began supplying its own correspondence instruction and had such success that in 1936 Arizona recognized the high school as the state center for correspondence instruction. Official recognition was accorded by the Arizona

State Department, state universities, school superintendents, and principals.

State Governments Meet Needs of Adults

The states have generally preferred to let each community run its own elementary and high school programs. State colleges, although founded and supported by state education departments, usually boast independent administrations. Gayle B. Childs summarized the role of state departments of education as follows:

> By and large, such departments conceive their functions to be advisory, administrative and supervisory, and while they provide assistance in the establishment and improvement of instructional programs, they do not, as a rule, engage in the actual process of instruction.[23]

Exceptions have arisen in cases in which students could participate in local programs and in the realm of continuing education for adults.

Massachusetts was one of the first states to set itself up as a supplier of correspondence instruction. The State Legislature in 1915 created the Extension Division within the Department of Education to provide education for adults. The program started with correspondence courses; extension classes were added later. The operation was unique in that "it was responsible not as in other states to a state university or to an equivalent state institution of higher education, but directly to the state Department of Education."[24] Teachers were obtained from the faculties of Massachusetts colleges, universities, institutes, and high schools. Funds for the program were appropriated by the State Legislature, but the Correspondence Course Program has been practically self-supporting.

The Correspondence Study Department of the Oregon State System of Higher Education was originally established in 1907 as part of the University of Oregon. In 1932 the department was placed under the General Extension Division (now the Division of Continuing Education) subject to the supervision of the State Board of Higher Education with funds allocated by the chancellor of the state system of education.

In an effort to provide an equal educational opportunity to geographically remote or homebound children, the state legislatures of North Dakota and Montana authorized supervised correspondence study programs in 1935 and 1939 respectively. North Dakota's program, now known as the Division of Supervised Study, offers primarily high school courses. Its full-time correspondence faculty provides not only courses but free testing and counseling services as well. An additional feature is a sizable lending library operated by the division. The Montana State Correspondence School, originally under the State Board of Education, served high school and elementary students, reaching a peak of over 1,250 enrollments in 1945–1946. But enrollment declined steadily thereafter, and the legislature finally cut off appropriations to the school between 1961 and 1963, thereby ensuring its termination.[25]

Alaska, a state which has a considerable problem with geographically remote students, has set up a correspondence instruction program for the eight elementary grades. The state department creates its own courses, based on texts used in the schools in the state system. High school courses by the University of Nebraska are the only ones approved for Alaska's students above the first eight grades who are beyond the range of bus transportation.[26]

U.S. Armed Forces Institute: Education for Military Personnel

The Army Institute was founded in 1941. In 1943 its services were extended to the other branches of the Armed Forces and its name was changed to the U.S. Armed Forces Institute (USAFI). Figure 2–2 shows the internal organizational structure of USAFI. The premise upon which the institute was founded remains unchanged: "that citizens in military uniform are interested in continuing their civilian education."[27]

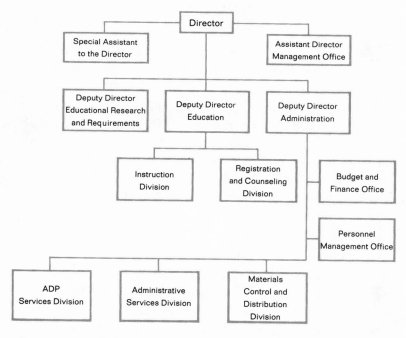

Figure 2–2   Internal organization of USAFI. (Source: Dr. Homer Kempfer, Director, U.S. Armed Forces Institute, Madison, Wis., December, 1967.)

USAFI does not engage in military training and is entirely separate from the instructional programs run by each of the Armed Forces for training purposes.[28] Although USAFI is under the supervision of the Department of Defense, its function is to provide nonmilitary educational opportunities for military personnel. The *Catalog of USAFI* defines the USAFI mission:

> It is the mission of USAFI to provide common services and materials by which the Army, Navy, Air Force, Marine Corps, and Coast Guard may supplement, for members of their commands, educational opportunities in subjects normally taught in civilian academic institutions, in order that the individual may render efficient service in his present assignment, increase his capabilities for assuming greater responsibility, and satisfy his intellectual desires.[29]

USAFI engages professional educators in the preparation of courses. By 1964 approximately two hundred correspondence courses were offered directly by USAFI in elementary, high school, college, and technical or vocational subjects; approximately six thousand other correspondence courses were made available to USAFI students through contract with the extension divisions of some forty participating colleges and universities.[30]

Religious Organizations

Religious organizations may offer correspondence instruction for one of three different motives: (1) to educate the layman who wants to enrich his life through Bible study or increase his effectiveness in his church; (2) to train ministers, missionaries, or laymen for church work; and (3) to proselyte and spread church doctrine. Readers will also remember that religious institutions were early experimenters in correspondence instruction through the work of Illinois Wesleyan University and Willam Rainey Harper's Correspondence School at Morgan Park.

Bible institutes serve many of the laymen who seek religious study through correspondence. The Correspondence School of the Moody Bible Institute was established in 1901 and is still in operation. The Emmaus Bible School runs a correspondence program which is particularly active in sending programs, translated into eighty different languages, overseas to 125 countries. The Correspondence School of the Lutheran Bible Institute not only serves the general public but provides free courses in some seventy penal institutions in the country. A recent survey by S. A. Witmer indicated the extent of correspondence teaching done by this kind of institute: "In the 1960 survey of Bible institutes and colleges in the United States and Canada, 32 schools reported home study departments with a total of 259,000 enrollees."[31]

The Department of Ministerial Education of the Methodist Church maintains over a dozen theological seminaries in the United States. Courses from the basic curriculum plus courses leading to a license to preach are made available to external students through the department's Correspondence Division.[32] The Baptist Church seminaries use correspondence instruction for continuing the education of ministers who have not completed college or seminary work.

PRIVATE INCENTIVE INTRODUCES
NEW SUPPLIERS (GENERAL CATEGORY)

CERP now passes from this review of how correspondence instruction grew within the framework of institutional education in the United States into the realm of private initiative. Universities and state governments, with their clearly defined educational goals and their well-established educational organizations, were able to plan ahead and use correspondence instruction to meet educational needs as they arose. But certain needs did not fit so neatly into the areas of concern and responsibility of existing educational institutions. The vacuum created by such unfulfilled needs eventually attracted both specialists and speculators interested in solving educational problems or recognizing the possibility of a profit. What were the stimuli which first encouraged the entry of private suppliers of correspondence instruction into the market?

Foster and the Mines

The reader will recall that Anna Eliot Ticknor set up the first correspondence study program in the United States in 1873. Inasmuch as her program was a private venture, Anna Ticknor may be said to have founded the first private home study school. But being the daughter of a professor and inclined toward charitable activity, Anna Ticknor never considered her school to be a private enterprise.

It was not until 1886 that the forerunner of the modern private home study school began operation. Its founder was a Civil War veteran, Thomas J. Foster, who published the *Shenandoah Herald* in the mining valleys of Pennsylvania.[33] Foster believed that hazardous conditions in the mines stemmed largely from ignorance of the principles of mine safety by owners, foremen, and miners. When Pennsylvania enacted a mine safety law in 1886, requiring mine foremen to pass state examinations, Foster decided to devote columns of his paper (by then called the *Mining Herald*) to questions and answers about mine safety. He also began printing pamphlets on accident prevention and published available data on the state examinations.

In 1888, Foster moved the *Herald* to Scranton and changed its name to *The Colliery Engineer,* thereby reflecting his paper's concern for mining problems. Widespread interest in his columns and pamphlets plus the obvious need for some instruction for miners prior to their taking the state examination led Foster to prepare more complete instructional materials. In 1891, with help from qualified engineers, he offered a correspondence course with a complete grading service to the public.[34]

The course was advertised in Foster's paper, and a fee that would bring in a profit was charged. Private incentive began serving the public by meeting an unfilled need with a well-prepared response. The very first enrollee, Thomas Coates, completed the course. In due time he became a mine superintendent and provided private home study schools with their first success story. Noffsinger described the reaction of industry to its first private correspondence course:

> The response it won from all men in the industry from those in the pits to superintendents led to the preparation of a more extended course and by the middle of 1892 there was an enrollment of more than a thousand. Inquiries came in for information from machinists, engineers, draftsmen and others employed in the mines and associated industries.[35]

The curriculum was expanded to meet additional training needs, eventually branching out beyond the limits of mining and adding new subjects. In 1901, the school was incorporated as the International Correspondence Schools (ICS), an organization still actively providing instruction.

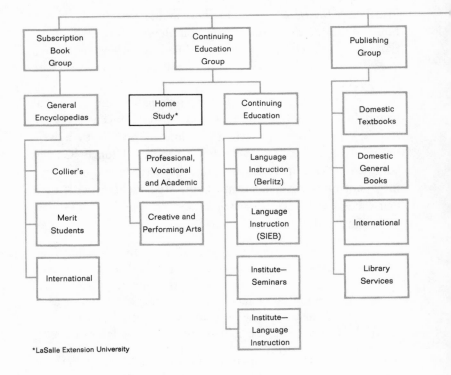

*LaSalle Extension University

Figure 2-3 Organization of Crowell Collier and Macmillan, Inc. and Subsidiaries (Source: Crowell Collier and Macmillan, Inc., New York, January, 1968.)

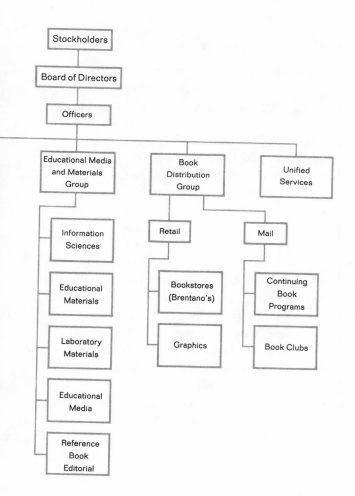

Other Early Vocational Suppliers

As school systems were still slow to react to industry's need for trained personnel at the turn of the century, other private ventures entered the supplier market. Most, like the American School, were formed to provide training opportunities for wage earners. The American School was granted a charter by the Commonwealth of Massachusetts in 1895 as a nonprofit training institution. In 1902 it moved to Chicago where it is still operating today as a private home study school under a nonprofit charter. American has offered a large number of vocational courses, mainly at the high school level and directed at adults or high school dropouts. "With its present enrollment of more than 100,000 students at all times, [American] represents what we believe to be the largest high school in the world from the standpoint of enrollment."[36]

The LaSalle Extension University, not to be confused with a conventional resident university, was one of the early correspondence instruction suppliers. It offered a variety of business courses—including accounting, management, office training—and a course in law. LaSalle still functions today, although it has been taken over and now operates as a division of the publisher Crowell Collier and Macmillan, Inc. (see Figure 2–3).

Calvert and Elementary Education

In correspondence instruction at the elementary school level, the name of the Calvert School stands out as the pioneer. Calvert offered correspondence instruction, at least experimentally, from its Baltimore resident institution, as early as

1905.[37] Virgil Hillyer, Calvert's director, described the system to the Third International Congress for Home Education, held in Brussels in 1910: *"Une école de Baltimore* [Calvert] *a créé en 1905 un système d'instruction à domicile par l'intermédia[i]re des parents ou des gouvernantes."*[38]*

Although Calvert had both resident and nonresident instructional programs to support, and although it had neither an endowment to cover operating expenditures nor support from government subsidies, its correspondence courses were not commercial in inspiration. In fact, for many years the home instruction department was a financial liability for the school. But as increasing mobility of American families enlarged the demand for a mobile form of education for elementary school pupils, economies of large-scale operation began to make the Calvert correspondence program more economically sound. Most of Calvert's competitors for the elementary education market in correspondence instruction are universities; the high cost and less lucrative profit possibilities have tended to make private suppliers shy away.

The Frauds

Before concluding the section on private incentive, CERP wishes to make it clear that not all private suppliers provide the quality instruction of a school such as Calvert. The possibilities for high profits have lured into correspondence instruction many suppliers who are looking for a fast dollar at little effort to themselves. Diploma mills offer substandard courses in everything from religion to technical matters. They pose a

---

* "A Baltimore school [Calvert] initiated in 1905 a system of home instruction with parents or tutors as intermediaries."

serious threat to all correspondence instruction suppliers. The problem of frauds will be treated in Chapter 3 in greater detail.

INCREASING EFFICIENCY THROUGH TRAINING
(TRAINING CATEGORY)

The organizations that use correspondence instruction to increase their efficiency of operation were the last of the three categories (education, general, and training) to enter the supplier market. Although businesses, professional and trade organizations, industrial concerns, the federal government, and the military all recognized the necessity for some kind of training program, they did not at first look to correspondence instruction to fill that need. Although some interest developed for training through correspondence instruction early in the twentieth century, it was not until World War I that interest began to pick up and be translated into correspondence instruction training programs.

Professional and Trade Associations

Professional and trade associations were the first of these organizations to use correspondence instruction intensively. Since many such organizations were founded expressly to establish or upgrade standards of performance among their members, providing instruction is naturally one of their chief functions. Training members, administering examinations, and recognizing member achievement are all activities still being carried out by professional and trade associations today.

The American Institute of Banking (AIB) was founded

by a group of Minneapolis bank employees who wanted to study banking systematically. In 1898, they met and engaged a teacher to hold evening classes. Two years later, the American Bankers Association (ABA) gave its official stamp to the AIB. A plan for taking the institute's training services to small banks in 1901 resulted in the formation of the Correspondence School of Banking. A report to the Executive Council of the ABA indicates that the association's Committee on Education held the correspondence program in high esteem:

> Your Committee would emphasize the importance of correspondence instruction. It overshadows, we believe, every other instrumentality that could be brought into operation. The organization of the bank clerks of the United States into chapters while attracting attention and apparently being of considerable moment, is, in the estimation of your Committee, of far less practical use than the work entered upon by the individual student along the lines in which he feels he is more or less deficient.[39]

Despite these advantages, the institute closed the correspondence study program after 3½ years. Although several other arrangements were tried, including a special agreement with International Correspondence Schools, it was not until 1942 that the correspondence program was returned to the institute, in which it still functions as part of the training operation.

The United Typothetae of America (UTA) was founded by a group of master printers in 1887. As part of the training program for apprentice and journeyman printers, the association provided correspondence instruction. Credit toward certification was granted upon course completion.

In 1930 the Insurance Institute of America investigated an interest in the use of correspondence instruction for preparing candidates for Insurance Institute examinations. In

1935, the International City Managers' Association established its Institute for Training in Municipal Administration. The association's training program was made available through correspondence instruction to local government employees. A correspondence study program for isolated members of the American Savings and Loan Institute (ASLI) was organized in 1934. A special feature of the ASLI program is its Group Home Study Plan, which combines individual correspondence instruction with group classes held by the institute.

The American Academy of Ophthalmology and Otolaryngology designed a course in 1940 for the M.D. who planned to practice, research, or teach in those specialties. The course was originated as a supplement to residency training for the medical school graduate, and annual enrollments have increased steadily. A more recent medical program is sponsored by the American Society of Abdominal Surgeons. In 1962, this organization began a correspondence course to provide continuing surgical education for the practicing surgeon. Although the society does not refer to its course as correspondence instruction, it provides the critical service of correcting, grading, and notifying the student of his results on questions that accompany course materials. Practicing surgeons serve as faculty members for the society's courses.

The American Dietetic Association instituted a correspondence course in 1959 to train personnel who serve under professionally qualified dietitians. It performs the interesting function of training nonprofessional food service supervisors (i.e., those outside the association) in hospitals and nursing homes to assume greater responsibilities, thus freeing the dietetic specialist to perform those duties for which only he is trained and qualified.

Business and Industry

Business and industry use correspondence instruction for a variety of purposes: to train workers, to supplement class instruction, and to follow up group training sessions. Many companies offer correspondence courses prepared externally under contract with other suppliers. Some companies also grant tuition refunds to employees studying through correspondence on their own incentive. But since CERP is interested primarily in business and industry as suppliers of correspondence instruction, the following survey will concern itself with companies actively engaged in supplying correspondence courses.

As increasingly complex machinery required increasingly skilled workmen, the apprentice system and shop-floor training program became insufficient. A massive need for rapid and professional training led to the formation of industry schools. Naturally enough, these training schools approached their task through the traditional classroom method.

> Since this was education the principles and methods adopted were those of the only kind of education with which we were familiar, that is, the principles and methods of public schools. In the first place, there was an automatic, unconscious selection. An additional reason lay in the fact that the first directors of education engaged by corporations were recruited from the public schools and colleges. They, of course, followed the only pedagogical principles and practices they knew. They adopted formal, classroom instruction as the method for imparting knowledge in the factory as in the classroom.[40]

Not until after World War I did many of these companies

begin turning to correspondence instruction to fill their training needs.

The Equitable Life Assurance Society was one of the first to introduce countrywide sales training through correspondence. A concentrated course, held at central locations, introduced trainees to the fundamentals of life insurance underwriting. This introduction to fundamentals was followed by a correspondence course which tied in with the agent's field practice. The program proved a success, and other companies followed suit. Connecticut Mutual Life, another early advocate of correspondence instruction, introduced it into their sales training program in 1920. New York Life began using correspondence instruction in 1952.

Sears, Roebuck and Company early developed several merchandising courses by correspondence instruction to supplement regular training materials issued to branch stores. Although most of the correspondence courses were eventually dropped when Sears developed enough trained personnel to handle training classes in large stores, the Sears Extension Institute still serves small stores in isolated regions.[41]

Westinghouse Electric conducted training programs for its employees as early as 1902. An extension division, relying primarily on correspondence instruction, was later created to train men in remote plants and offices. Western Electric, another early experimenter in employee training programs, used apprenticeship, evening classes, vestibule schools, and training institutes before finally establishing, in 1958, both basic and advanced correspondence courses as adjuncts to its Graduate Engineering Training Correspondence Study Program.

Standard Oil Company had developed an extensive training system for its New York office prior to 1930. The core of the program was the Regular Petroleum Curriculum, a series of eight consecutive courses requiring four years for completion. Because of enthusiasm for the course, Standard Oil decided to test its appeal through correspondence. When enrollment was sufficiently high, students were expected to gather at regular intervals to form discussion groups under the supervision of a company-supplied group leader.

Labor Unions

Labor unions have, on the whole, been uninterested in the use of correspondence instruction. Although labor unions often carry out instructional programs, both to train workers and to indoctrinate them in union procedures and encourage union loyalty, very few use the correspondence method.

In 1921, the Workers Education Bureau of America (WEB) was organized to stimulate education within the labor unions. Although WEB was not within the structure of organized labor, in 1923 the American Federation of Labor (AFL) designated it as an approved agency and later began giving it moderate financial support. Correspondence instruction was one of WEB's standard instructional methods.

The International Typographical Union (ITU) has one of the oldest apprentice programs involving correspondence instruction. (The reader will recall that master printers of the United Typothetae of America had used correspondence instruction in their training program as early as 1887.) In 1908, an agreement between the ITU and the Inland Printer Technical School of Chicago provided a series of thirty-six correspondence lessons in printing craftsmanship for union members and apprentices. During World War I the union prepared its own courses and began demanding compulsory enrollment of apprentices. Every ITU member, in particular, had to complete the course on trade unionism.

The Boiler Makers Union is another of the active suppliers of correspondence instruction. It requires all apprentices to enroll in an externally supplied correspondence course for the purpose of upgrading members of the building and metal trades.

Federal Government

The federal government has used correspondence instruction to train employees in several of its specialized agencies. The instructional motives have generally been to train new workers, to introduce skilled workers into the routine of government service, and to standardize agency practice around the country.

The Internal Revenue Service (IRS) established a Branch of Correspondence Study in 1919 to provide IRS employees with training in IRS activities.[42] Although correspondence instruction is now being partially phased out by the IRS, it probably will continue to be used as an instructional supplement.[43]

In 1945, the Federal Aviation Agency (FAA) Academy developed a directed (home) study program. Figure 2–4 orients the Directed Study Section in the FAA complex. By its special term *directed study*, the FAA means correspondence instruction coupled with on-the-job training and post-residence review. The correspondence instruction is used to prepare electronic technicians for concentrated periods of advanced resident training.

The Selective Service System began preparation of correspondence courses in 1948. Information and experience gathered during the drafting of millions of Americans in World War II was used to organize ten courses for civilians and military personnel affiliated with the selective service. Courses range from instruction in handling selective service forms to the more complex matter of dependency deferment.[44]

Although the Post Office Department is over two hundred years old, training needs of its employees were not recognized until after its decentralization in 1954. The Seattle regional office designated a ten-lesson home study program, but it provided none of the necessary features of correspondence instruction. However, the Denver regional office established a correspondence program for in-service training of employees in 1963, including feedback of teachers' evaluation of student lessons.

The federal government does supply one correspondence program which, in contrast to its general practice, provides instructional opportunities that extend to users beyond the employees of the supplying agency. Since 1921, the Department of Agriculture has run its own graduate school. Yet it receives no federal funds, grants no degrees, and is not even an official part of the department. A general administrative board runs the school, which offers a correspondence program that is both nonprofit and self-supporting. Correspondence instruction is used to extend the graduate school's services to field employees of government agencies. About three-fourths of the twenty-three courses offer credits applicable to civil service eligibility requirements.

Armed Forces

The Armed Forces, although relative latecomers in accepting the use of correspondence instruction, are today the country's

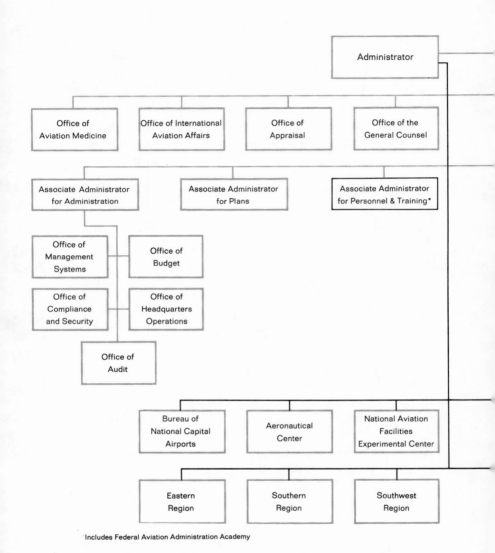

Includes Federal Aviation Administration Academy

Figure 2–4   Internal organization of Federal Aviation Administration. (Source: Adapted from a chart furnished by Federal Aviation

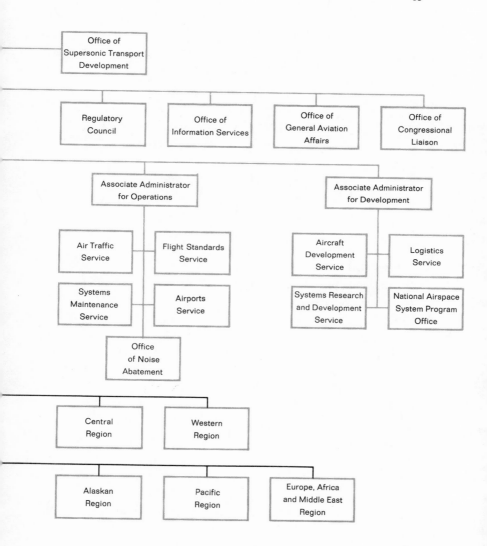

Administration, now a part of the Department of Transportation, 1967.)

largest suppliers. Training is related directly to career progress in the military, providing built-in incentive for the student. Instruction is usually based upon courses given in resident service schools and is distributed free to students.

The Army began experimenting with correspondence instruction after World War I. Satisfaction with the results spurred expansion of correspondence programs. By 1958, the Army was offering well over eleven hundred different military subcourses by correspondence instruction.

The Navy, through the Naval War College, initiated its first correspondence course in 1914. There now exist correspondence courses to cover every phase of officer training and rating of enlisted personnel. The heavy demand for these courses led to a partial decentralization of the Navy's correspondence service. The Naval Correspondence Course Center in Scotia, New York, administers the correspondence instruction of officers, reserves, and enlisted men at small commands; commands with more than four officers are responsible for grading and certifying the completion of courses taken by active-duty personnel. Both military and civilian personnel staff the Scotia center.

Correspondence instruction originated in the Air Force as an extension service of the Army Continental Air Command. When the Air Force became a separate branch of the Armed Forces in 1947, the U.S. Air Force Extension (correspondence) Course Department was organized. In 1950, the program was reorganized under the Air University as the USAF Extension Course Institute (ECI) at Gunter Air Force Base, Alabama.[45] ECI's task was defined as:

> . . . providing off-duty, self-study military education and vocational training for both active and reserve components by extending . . . capabilities of Air Force resident schools to

eligible personnel in the field; the ECI provides a means for Air Force personnel to sustain their career progress when they cannot attend resident courses or where resident courses do not apply or are not available.[46]

Correspondence is now an integral part of career advancement training in the Air Force. The meticulous definition of task in the Air Force can be seen in Figure 2–5, which shows the institute in its supportive position surrounded by other components of the Air University.

The Marine Corps Institute began its correspondence operation by supplying courses for enlisted Marines in 1920. During World War II it began preparing high school, junior college, and vocational courses, but by 1954 this program was being replaced by specific career development courses intended primarily for enlisted Marines.

The Coast Guard, operating under the Treasury Department, relied exclusively on resident centers and on-the-job training until 1928. When the Coast Guard Institute (CGI) was organized in that year, it was regarded as a supplementary training supplier. After several moves, the CGI became a division of the Coast Guard Training Center at Groton, Connecticut, in 1964. Although it originally limited its correspondence program to training directly related to Coast Guard duties, CGI eventually added some academic courses.

However, with the founding of the U.S. Armed Forces Institute in 1942, the CGI began terminating these educational courses.[47] All branches of the services came to rely on USAFI for providing educational courses and turned their own resources strictly to military training needs.

The Industrial College of the Armed Forces operates for all the services. Its graduate-level correspondence program, opened in 1950, is available to all officers of major or lieuten-

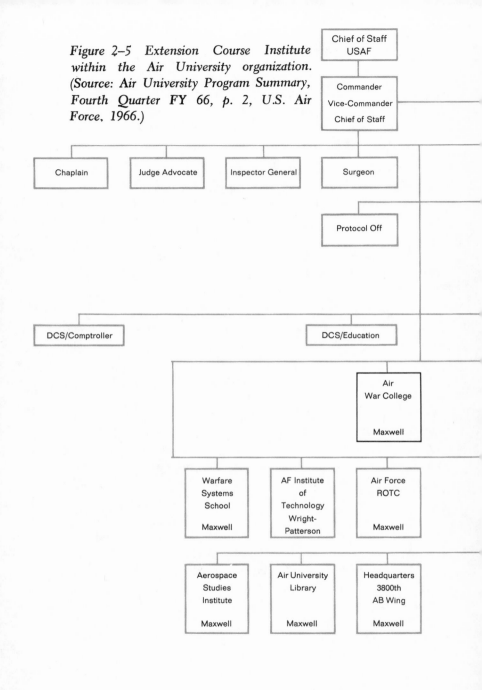

Figure 2–5 Extension Course Institute within the Air University organization. (Source: Air University Program Summary, Fourth Quarter FY 66, p. 2, U.S. Air Force, 1966.)

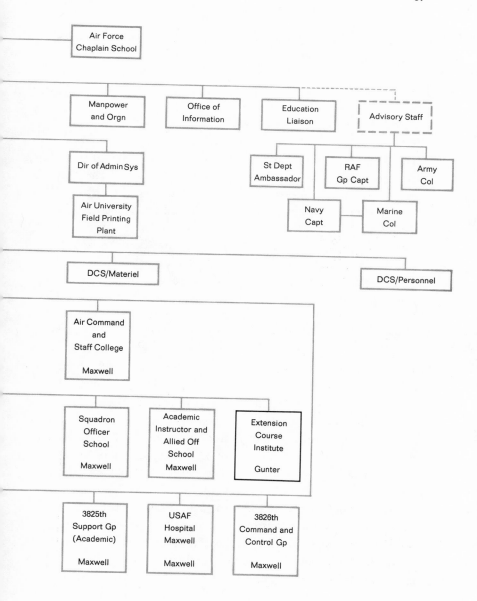

ant commander grade or higher in the Department of Defense and the Coast Guard. Some high-level government employees and civilian executives are also eligible.

SUMMARY

The American educational system experienced a critical period of growth and development over the second half of the nineteenth century. The push to provide a truly equal educational opportunity for all created some problems that seemed beyond the capabilities of the existing system. As educators became aware of these problems, they began applying Yankee ingenuity and frontier optimism to overcoming them.

Correspondence instruction proved to be one of the solutions they developed. It helped the universities, state and local governments, religious institutions, and the federal government (through USAFI and the Graduate School of the Department of Agriculture) serve the educational needs of those who were unable to take advantage of resident education. It helped professional associations, big business, industrial concerns, the federal government, and the Armed Forces fill their demands for trained personnel. And it helped private home study schools offer instruction to individuals who were unable to participate in other programs or who chose to satisfy their own needs or wishes through correspondence study.

Acceptance of the method was slow. Started by the daughter of a Harvard professor for a small group of followers in 1873, the method now reaches an estimated three million students every year. For some suppliers, correspondence instruction merely plugs gaps in cases in which other methods of instruction are impractical. Others swear by the method and use it for instruction in matters vital to the individual's, company's, or even the nation's welfare.

CERP considers the problems that stimulated the creation of correspondence instruction extremely important in determining how the method developed in acceptance and stature. This development, in turn, will help explain many of the problems that face correspondence suppliers today. CERP has gone into considerable detail in describing the early uses and suppliers of correspondence instruction because they form the foundation for the operation of the method. Financing a correspondence instruction venture, selecting a staff, attracting or screening out students, creating a favorable image, and operating successfully within institutional limitations—these are all activities correspondence suppliers must carry out in addition to their basic task of supplying instruction. They are linked to our country's past, to its educational traditions, and to the traditions that have been built up within the confines of correspondence instruction. The problems they impose on the supplier provide the topic for Chapter 3.

NOTES

1. Adolphe Meyer, *An Educational History of the Western World* (New York: McGraw Hill Book Company, 1965), p. 456.

2. Robert D. Strom, *The Tragic Migration* (Washington, D.C.: National Education Association, 1964), p. 2.

3. J. S. Noffsinger, "The Story of the Benton Harbor Plan," *First International Conference on Correspondence Education*, Victoria, British Columbia, Aug. 22–24, 1938, p. 82.

4. Nathaniel Peffer, *Educational Experiments in Industry* (New York: The Macmillan Company, 1932), pp. 4–5.

5. *First International Conference on Correspondence Education*, Victoria, British Columbia, Aug. 22–24, 1938, p. 10.

6. "Supervised Correspondence Study," report on conference held at Teachers College, Columbia University, New York (Scranton, Pa.: International Textbook Company, 1934), p. 3.

7. *Catalog 1964–65*, Division of Supervised Study, North Dakota State University, Fargo, p. 2.

8. Alfred L. Hall-Quest, *The University Afield* (New York: The Macmillan Company, 1926), p. 8.

9. Walton S. Bittner and Hervey F. Mallory, *University Teaching by Mail* (New York: The Macmillan Company, 1933), p. 12.

10. George Ticknor introduced elective courses into Harvard College and was a founder and president of the Boston Public Library.

11. "The Correspondence University," *Harper's Weekly*, vol. 27 (Oct. 27, 1883), p. 635.

12. *Ibid.*, p. 675.

13. Thomas W. Goodspeed, *William Rainey Harper* (Chicago: The University of Chicago Press, 1928), p. 53.

14. *Ibid.*, p. 69.

15. John H. Vincent, *The Chautauqua Movement* (Boston: Chautauqua Press, 1886), pp. 183, 194.

16. Joseph E. Gould, *The Chautauqua Movement* (New York: The State University of New York, 1961), p. 30.

17. Goodspeed, *op. cit.*, p. 112.

18. W. H. Lighty, "Correspondence-study Teaching," *Educational Review*, vol. 51 (January, 1916), p. 42.

19. *Proceedings of the First National University Extension Conference,* Madison, Wis., 1915, p. 15.

20. "Supervised Correspondence Study," *loc. cit.*

21. Noffsinger, *op. cit.,* pp. 82–89.

22. J. S. Noffsinger, "Institutional Development," *Phi Delta Kappan,* vol. 22 (December, 1939), p. 190.

23. G. B. Childs, "State Agencies in a Program of Supervised Correspondence Instruction," *The Bulletin of the National Association of Secondary-School Principals,* vol. 36 (December, 1952), p. 97.

24. James A. Moyer, "Adult Education," *Phi Delta Kappan,* vol. 22 (December, 1939), p. 196.

25. Letter to CERP from Harriet Miller, State Superintendent, Department of Public Instruction, Helena, Mont., Aug. 19, 1964.

26. Letters to CERP from Robert P. Isaac, Special Assistant, Department of Education, Juneau, Alaska, Sept. 25, 1964 and Sept. 1, 1967.

27. Ripley S. Sims, "Writing the USAFI Correspondence Course" (Madison, Wis.: U.S. Armed Forces Institute, 1960), p. 5.

28. Military programs are surveyed separately.

29. *Catalog of USAFI,* U.S. Armed Forces Institute, Washington, D.C., Sept. 10, 1963, p. 5.

30. CERP interview with Wilbur Brothers, Deputy Director, USAFI, and H. F. Cromer, Assistant Director of Education, USAFI, Aug. 24, 1964.

31. S. A. Witmer, *The Bible College Story: Education with Dimension* (Manhasset, N.Y.: Channel Press, Inc., 1962), pp. 125–126.

32. Connolly C. Gamble, Jr., *The Continuing Theological Education of the American Minister* (Richmond, Va.: Union Theo-

logical Seminary, 1960), p. 52. In 1959 there were approximately six thousand ministerial student enrollees in the correspondence program.

33. *The ICS Story* (Scranton, Pa.: International Correspondence Schools, n.d.), p. 1.

34. *Ibid.*, pp. 1–5.

35. J. S. Noffsinger, *Correspondence Schools, Lyceums, Chautauquas* (New York: The Macmillan Company, 1926), p. 12.

36. *Bulletin of the American School* (Chicago: American School, 1963), p. 6.

37. Archibald Hart, *Calvert and Hillyer, 1897–1947* (Baltimore: Waverly Press, Inc., 1947), p. 56.

38. *Ibid.*

39. Richard W. Hill and Marion Turner, *Fifty Years of Banking Education* (New York: American Institute of Banking, 1950), p. 37.

40. Peffer, *op. cit.*, p. 9.

41. Panel report quoting Harry L. Wellbank, National Training Director, Sears, Roebuck and Company, *Proceedings of the Conference on the Teaching of Scientific and Technical Subjects by Correspondence*, University of Illinois, Urbana (October, 1958), pp. 54–55.

42. "A Brief History of the Training Function in the Internal Revenue Service," Department of the Treasury, Washington, D.C., (n.d.), pp. 5–7. (Mimeographed.)

43. Interview with George T. Reeves, Jr., Director, Training Division, Internal Revenue Service, Nov. 11, 1964.

44. *Catalog of Correspondence Courses*, Field Division, National Headquarters, Selective Service System, Washington, D.C., 1962.

45. Harold F. Clark and Harold S. Sloan, *Classrooms in the*

Military (New York: Teachers College, Columbia University, 1964), p. 73.

46. "Extracts from ECI Historical Reports" (n.d.), p. 2. (Mimeographed.)

47. See earlier section on USAFI in this chapter.

3

Problems (External) of the
Correspondence Instruction
Supplier

SUPPLIERS of correspondence instruction face two distinct kinds of problems: external and internal. In Chapter 3, CERP examines those problems external to the actual teaching function. Although outside the exchange of materials and the student-teacher interaction that define the correspondence method, such problems still directly affect the supplier's ability to provide quality instruction. Internal problems—difficulties inherent in the method as a means of instruction—will be treated at length in Chapter 4, in which CERP analyzes the advantages and disadvantages of the correspondence method.

Four main problems make up Chapter 3: (1) financing, (2) maintaining a quality staff, (3) defining the correspondence student, and (4) gaining acceptance of correspondence instruction. These problems are closely interrelated. Financial considerations affect a supplier's ability to obtain staff and attract students; all these, in turn, affect the supplier's public image.

In the past, critics and commentators have tended to lump these external problems together with problems of the instructional method. CERP separates the two in order to demonstrate their basic disparity. Although external problems may impinge strongly on instruction, they are basically administrative problems and their solutions must be administrative, not instructional.

FINANCING

CERP course reviewers report that many correspondence courses are not as good as they could be. They suggest one reason is that adequate resources are not being allocated to the task of supplying good correspondence instruction. The quality of a program depends, at least in part, on how well it is financed; good course writers, carefully prepared materials, and qualified instructors and graders are expensive.

A CERP survey asked correspondence program directors to rank their five most serious operational problems. Their responses indicate a great diversity among suppliers. Combined statistics from all respondents indicate that "lack of funds" is the correspondence supplier's fourth greatest problem. It falls below "motivating students," "obtaining qualified graders," and "obtaining qualified teachers." However, all three of the higher-ranked problems and many of the lower-ranked ones depend, at least partially, on available funds.

Some administrators claim to have few or no direct financial problems, while others must devote much of their time, energy, and ingenuity to collecting funds. Representatives of the Armed Forces do not list a need for funds among their problem, although correspondence instruction directors in industry rate the need for funds lowest among their problems. Oddly enough, university correspondence administrators do not place financial difficulties among their five ranked problems, yet most of their ranked problems stem from a lack of finances. On the other hand, private home study school directors consider obtaining funds to be their third most pressing problem, although correspondence instruction directors in professional and trade associations list it as problem number one. One can see from this distribution that finance is one of the key variables among correspondence instruction operations. CERP feels that the lack of resources is a more serious problem than some suppliers have admitted.

In-House Training Suppliers: a Practical Approach

Since most of the suppliers who use correspondence instruction for training their own people do so in their own self-interest, they tend to allocate the financial support necessary to carry out effective programs. The employer who chooses correspondence instruction as the best way to train his employees in necessary skills knows that he will not get a satisfactory return on his investment unless the method is effective. Thus he is unlikely to hamstring his program with insufficient funds.

ARMED FORCES Military budgets for correspondence instruction are deceptive. Military salaries are paid from a centralized single appropriation. Overhead expenses, housing, utilities, vehicles, and even postage are often buried in the cost of running the military installation where the correspondence operation is located. The main items that appear on correspondence program budgets in the Armed Forces are direct costs, but not even all these appear.

The Naval Correspondence Course Center at Scotia, New York, provides a good illustration of the complexity of finances behind a military correspondence operation. The center receives an annual budget of $725,000, but this accounts for only one-third of the cost of operation. A more complete list of supporting funds includes:

1. The $725,000 budget appropriation, much of which pays civil service employees and covers office expenses

2. $450,000 per year in military costs, such as pay of military personnel

3. A large sum to cover postage, a major expenditure

4. Rent, utilities, and custodial pay, which amount to $112,000 per year

5. Miscellaneous costs including vehicles and equipment, valued at $8,000 annually[1]

Because of its importance to national defense, training in the Armed Forces receives adequate funds with little controversy. The combined Armed Forces allocated $3 billion for its training program in 1964, a whopping amount by any standard. Major items were technical training, recruit training, and flight training. Correspondence instruction shared in the $374 million allotted to other training needs. The correspondence programs of the Armed Forces typically spend approximately 75 percent of their allotted budget on materials and services directly related to instruction. No persuasive literature or promotional campaigns divert funds from the process of instruction. No fees are involved as courses are distributed without cost to servicemen.

BUSINESS AND INDUSTRY One correspondence instruction authority estimates that of the approximately $4.5 to $5 billion that business and industry invest yearly in training programs, no more than $10 to $15 million gets channeled into correspondence instruction.[2] Corporations spend this two- or three-tenths of 1 percent of their total training budgets on the following:

1. Correspondence courses purchased from outside suppliers such as universities or private home study schools

2. Courses taken independently by employees from outside suppliers under tuition refund plans

3. Correspondence courses created and supplied directly by the company, usually free to employees

One hundred and eight companies in a CERP survey, or 43 percent of those indicating that they use correspondence instruction, grant tuition refunds to employees studying by correspondence. In another survey of 155 companies (taken by the National Industrial Conference Board in 1956), 63 percent stipulated that rebates are granted only in cases in which resident instruction is not available.

FEDERAL GOVERNMENT, LABOR UNIONS, AND PROFESSIONAL AND TRADE ASSOCIATIONS Federal government training programs operate essentially from federal appropriations. The Graduate School of the Department of Agriculture, however, receives no financial support from the government.

The International Typographical Union supports its correspondence instruction of apprentices with union funds. Supplementary funds come from the $35 each apprentice pays to take the course. The union also includes a per capita tax payment which the apprentice pays for *not* taking the correspondence courses if he is exempt through previous training or experience.

Professional and trade associations derive operating funds from membership dues, initiation fees, or membership deposits. Additional fees are often charged for individual courses taken by correspondence.

Suppliers of Educational Instruction: Differing Degrees of Support

Educational suppliers of correspondence instruction generally have greater difficulty than training suppliers in financing their operations. The rapidly growing demand for education keeps constant pressure on the resources available to educational institutions. Many institutions are reluctant to accept correspondence instruction and hesitate to allot it adequate financial support. The various instructional methods must compete for federal, state, or university funds, and correspondence instruction is frequently pushed aside by the more conventional demands on educational resources.

U.S. ARMED FORCES INSTITUTE (USAFI) USAFI is one notable exception. USAFI receives a direct appropriation from the Department of Defense. In 1965, the institute accounted for a budget of nearly $5.6 million. This does not include the $5 matriculation fee, paid by the student upon registering for his initial USAFI course, which reverts to a general fund in the U.S. Treasury. Approximately 79 percent of the USAFI budget goes directly into instruction—course preparation and operation, participating college program, testing, and dependents' schools program—while the remaining 21 percent is designated for administration and plant operation. It is interesting to note that USAFI keeps an inventory worth from $1 million to $2.5 million in educational supplies at all times. Experience has shown that USAFI must keep an inventory worth approximately 75 percent of the annual issue to students in order to meet its demands.

STATE GOVERNMENTS The states that supply correspondence instruction give their correspondence departments varying degrees of financial support. Funds for Oregon's correspondence study department are budgeted by the Division on Continuing Education and are augmented by student fees. The Massachusetts Legislature appropriates between $275,000 and $300,000 annually to cover permanent salaries and permits the Extension Division of the Massachusetts Department of Education to use up to $400,000 from correspondence course sales receipts to cover all other expenditures. Within the division, the supervisor of correspondence receives an extremely limited budget. Yet even though three out of five enrollments are free—war veterans, servicemen stationed in Massachusetts, the blind, senior citizens, hospital patients, and prison inmates are all entitled to correspondence instruction without charge—the program has been practically self-supporting.[3] The North Dakota State Legislature grants direct appropriations to support that state's Division of Supervised Study. North Dakota requires a $1 initial registration fee but provides courses free to state residents thereafter. The correspondence study department in Alaska receives its funds from the Department of Education.

PHILANTHROPIC AND RELIGIOUS SUPPLIERS Some organizations which exist primarily for charitable or civic purposes supply correspondence instruction. The John Tracy Clinic and the Hadley School for the Blind are two well-known examples. Such organizations rely largely on private sources of income or public subscription or, more rarely, on government grants to support their operation.

Religious suppliers of correspondence instruction receive grants from denominational boards, subsidies from religious college or seminary general funds, and fees from students. But student fees are not a dependable source of income for many of these groups as the fee is often determined by the student's ability to pay. Many such suppliers continue the correspondence service when fees are not paid. Even when fees are conscientiously submitted, a review of the catalogs of religious correspondence instruction programs reveals that typical charges range only from $1 to $10.

A large part of the financial support for correspondence instruction programs sponsored by philanthropic or religious institutions comes in the form of hidden subsidies: the work of faithful missionaries, teachers, and laymen who contribute time and services to the development and operation of correspondence courses. One director, suggesting that his program operated without sufficient funds, explained that his school had been able to translate several correspondence courses into eighty-one different languages with only a slight drain on a modest budget. This was accomplished with the help of numerous volunteers. It is not difficult to find one of these correspondence schools operating on a budget of $15,000. Because such schools are often partially supported by some parent institution, they can apply a large percentage of their budgeted funds to instructional materials and services.

UNIVERSITIES AND COLLEGES   The role of the university in society has long been a controversial subject in the academic community. Some claim that the university has a primary responsibility to further knowledge through scholarly research and to train an elite to carry on this activity; opponents claim that the university best serves society by bringing comprehensive learning to the people. Unfortunately, too limited resources—qualified teachers and administrators as well as funds—produce a conflict among educators seeking to distribute them as effectively as possible.

The proponents of the "elite" viewpoint reach back to the European tradition of the university as a research center. They see the extension of university responsibilities as a grave threat. "Many sincere and dedicated university leaders . . . regard adult education with uneasy suspicion. They dread the possibility that the hordes of new claimants on their time and service may finally destroy the university itself."[4] In 1891, when the University of Wisconsin faculty approved the adoption of a correspondence program, administrators included the following stipulation:

> Such courses shall not involve the University in any expense. Professors shall undertake only so much work of this class as can be done without serious injury to their regular duties in the University.[5]

The controversial economist and scholar, Thorstein Veblen, was among the most vehement critics of extending university responsibility. He felt extension programs detracted from the essential research function of the university and provided a service of dubious quality and utility:

> A variety of "university extension" bureaux have . . . been installed, to comfort and edify the unlearned with lyceum

lectures, to dispense erudition by mail-order, and to maintain some putative contact with amateur scholars and dilettanti beyond the pale.[6]

Abraham Flexner, an even more vitriolic critic of universities engaged in activities which he termed "business, not education," struck out bitterly against their undertaking correspondence instruction.

Now, correspondence courses may have their uses; and in a country where postage is cheap and superficiality rampant, they are likely to spring up; but that the prestige of the University of Chicago should be used to bamboozle well-meaning but untrained persons with the notion that they can thus receive a high school or a college education is scandalous. It is only fair to say that resentment is rife among the genuine scholars and scientists on the faculties of Columbia, Chicago, and other institutions.[7]

Flexner felt that such activity was turning the university into a "service station"; high school courses, agricultural extension activities, and nonacademic or vocational programs, he claimed, are not university responsibilities and needlessly dissipate all-too-scarce university resources.

But many who support taking higher learning to the populace find these critics too narrow in their attitudes. They argue that resident institutions can never meet all the the country's educational demands and that the goal of providing an equal educational opportunity for all justifies extending the university beyond its research function. Despite criticism from the Veblens and the Flexners, the liberal service function of the university is increasingly accepted today and continues to direct a small part of the scarce university resources toward correspondence instruction.

Originally universities established correspondence instruction programs with the assumption that they would be self-supporting. Today, however, funds from university appropriations typically supplement student fees. Sometimes state legislatures or private organizations assist universities in financing particular programs. In some cases, state law or university policy requires the correspondence director to return fees to a state treasury or university general fund. In CERP interviews, university correspondence directors complain that such practices hamper their activities, and they urge greater financial support for their operations.

Most of the university correspondence programs affiliated with the National University Extension Association (NUEA) have received substantial budget and fee income increases over the past thirty years. Although some NUEA departments as well as several non-NUEA departments operate on budgets of less than $100,000, many fall into the $100,000 to $250,000 category. One university correspondence center made expenditures of over $500,000 in 1964–1965.

As in USAFI, many university correspondence departments receive disguised subsidies in the form of rent-free facilities, central printing and mailing facilities, and sometimes a salaried staff supported by the university. In such circumstances, an excess of tuition income over expenditure does not necessarily indicate a net profit to the university.

Tuition fees and university subsidies provide the main sources of income for these correspondence programs. Usually a flat rate per credit hour is arbitrarily charged in all courses. A review of 1964–1965 catalogs shows that tuition rates tend to cluster around $10 to $12.50 per semester of college credit. The extremes, representing only a few universities, range from $7 to $30 per credit. In addition, students sometimes pay a small examination fee, a materials fee, a service charge, and infrequently a matriculation fee. High school courses, rated in terms of Carnegie units, cost the student from $21 to $36 per unit and $12 to $22 per half unit for state residents.

Suppliers of General Instruction: Education for a Profit

CERP examines here only those private home study schools which are in the business to make a profit.

The profit motive in education has come under heavy fire from educational traditionalists. They fear that concern for profit may lead to greater promotional costs, shortcuts to teaching and grading, and consequently to shabbier instruction and a general relaxation of standards. Private home study spokesmen, for their part, reject the implication that there is something sinister about earning a profit from education. Why, they ask, should society approve medical care for profit and condemn profit in education? They further point out that no one complains about teaching how to fly an airplane or play the guitar for profit. The tradition of laissez faire should operate in education just as it does elsewhere, they maintain.

Those who approve of permitting private home study on a commercial basis contend that competition helps to raise standards and that poor programs are forced out of business because of bad reputations and customer dissatisfaction. But at the same time they admit that competition leads to high promotional and sales costs and diversion of a large part of the program budget from the essential process of instruction.

Someone must pay for education. If the student does not pay directly for his courses, taxpayers pay for them indirectly by taxes. Private home study directors feel that the whole question of profit is merely a matter of semantics. They point out that it costs the taxpayer about twice as much to keep a student in public high school for one year as it does to provide him with an entire high school education by correspondence. Opponents say this argument begs the question: they criticize the profit motive, not the total cost of instructional programs.

Critics find fault with a system in which, in order to keep the high enrollment figures needed to ensure a profit, most private home study schools must plow a large part of their budget into advertising and sales promotion. This practice necessarily reduces the funds available for creating and servicing high-quality courses. Directors of private home study schools argue that these costs parallel university expenditure on resident facilities and serve an important purpose. The president of one correspondence school claims:

> Our investment in a physical plant is relatively minimal. This is true (on a relative basis) of all home study schools. That means the campus is not a "sales tool" as it is for a college or university. To a large extent, we rely on advertising to take our story to our prospective students rather than have our campus draw students to it. . . . While the pathway to degree-granting institutions is today well defined and accepted, the opportunities existing for those who cannot go to college are not equally well defined. Thus, the private home study school must seek out those who can and should increase their education. . . . I urge that we have a responsibility to the public to do this.[8]

In his book on adult education, Lyman Bryson phrased the argument slightly differently:

> Promotion and publicity are necessary even in the advancement of a self-directed activity, because freedom of choice is as much limited by ignorance as by anything else. No one can choose to do something which he has never heard of doing. It is

nonsense to say that people do not wish to do things which they have never been offered a chance to do. Promotion in adult education is essentially an invitation to inspect a program.[9]

However, encouraging high enrollment raises the problem of the nonstart and the dropout. The former is the student who enrolls for a course but never submits the first lesson; the latter is the student who begins a course but does not complete it. Resident institutions have counseling programs to assist and encourage students in difficulty, but few private home study schools are willing—many argue it is not feasible—to offer adequate counseling services to a diffuse student body. As a result, many students do not complete courses for which they contrac:. This raises several financial problems. For example, should a student receive a refund for a course he does not complete? It is important to remember that when a student enrolls for a course, he signs a legally binding contract. Schools accredited by the National Home Study Council (NHSC) give pro rata refunds according to the stringent rules of the NHSC.[10]

The typical private home study school predicts the number of dropouts and nonstarts and adjusts its budget accordingly. Some of these schools refuse to reimburse nonstarts or dropouts at all. Promotional costs run so high for some suppliers that they operate on a marginal budget for instructional services. There unfortunately exist many private home study schools whose sales and promotional expenditures are so great that the schools cannot make a profit without the phenomenon of dropouts. These schools realize that they must "oversell" their product in order to show a profit but justify this by saying that all the students *could* profit from the courses. No one questions the right of anyone to buy a textbook, they argue, so why should anyone demand selective selling of study programs?

The answer lies perhaps in sales technique and emphasis.

A CERP survey shows that medium-sized private home study schools spend an estimated 40 to 45 percent of their total expenditure on sales and promotion. Direct instructional costs in such schools account for only about 17 percent of the budget outlay. It is not unusual for a leading school to offer $14,000 to $18,000 to an experienced salesman for enrolling students who respond to advertising campaigns. During 1965, one large school spent $8.7 million on advertising, selling, and promotion. The Massachusetts Legislative Research Council voiced strong criticism of such practices:

> The large sums spent to obtain enrollments are criticized as a bad aspect of the correspondence school system of education and this criticism has considerable force. Thus, in the better schools, an average of 35 percent of student fees is necessary to promote sales; in the inferior institutions, this ratio may range as high as 65 percent.[11]

The better schools argue that economies of scale developed through large enrollments permit them to offer broader and better instructional programs. But to obtain high enrollments, some schools frequently have to resort to "hard sell" techniques or even misleading offers. Even the good private home study schools are caught in the circular trap of competition and advertising. Student enrollments are essential to their continued existence. To attract students being sought avidly by competing schools, they must advertise and promote their product. One zealous director, in explaining his school's advertising in pulp magazines, compared it to a clergyman going to skid row for converts.

The operating revenue of private home study schools is supplied entirely from student tuition fees. In 1924, Noffsinger estimated that $70 million was received annually by these schools. He noted that this sum exceeded the combined total educational expenditure of fourteen states in that same year.[12] Since that time, private home study instruction has grown into an even bigger business, taking in over twice that sum. The Massachusetts Legislative Research Council Report quotes the Russell Sage Foundation Report and an NHSC press release in commenting on the inadequacy of the $70 million figure still appearing in 1960 as authoritative:

> Based on the Russell Sage Foundation Report of 1939 a considerably higher estimate is suggested of the financial significance of private correspondence schools. With an estimated 1,500,000 pupils enrolled in 1960 in these private schools, the total revenue in fees approximates a minimum of $150,000,000.[13]

This seems to be a realistic minimum as the reported revenue from only seven of the larger schools in 1965 was $79.4 million. This figure far exceeds the tuition and fee income of all university correspondence departments combined.

Average tuition fees at private home study schools range from the $10 to $50 category up to the $300 to $600 category to as much as $1,000 for an engineering course extending over several years. Tuition is determined by several variables including the cost of preparing and servicing the course and the school's estimate of what price the market will bear. Students may often pay for the more expensive courses on an installment plan. In general, course fees in private home study schools are not out of line—if promotional costs and noncompletions are considered acceptable. Their net profits ranging from 4 to 12 percent are reasonable by standards of the American business economy.

Some of these schools are proprietary or single-owner schools. The relative ease of entry into the supplier market and the low capital outlay needed to begin operation make it possible for small schools to operate on shoestring budgets. But CERP is primarily concerned with the schools that handle the bulk of instruction. Most of these are incorporated. Of the seventy-seven schools belonging to the National Home Study Council in 1966, four issue stock that is publicly traded and held. Only fifty-nine organizations control the seventy-seven schools, and of these only one is a partnership and not one is a sole proprietorship. In 1966, four of the prominent accredited schools were listed in the *Million Dollar Directory* as having an estimated net worth of over $1 million.[14]

Perhaps private home study suppliers are right when they object that critics place too much emphasis on the question of profit. They point out that self-supporting university correspondence departments meet the same problems, often in the same manner. These departments—especially those with no-refund policies—also profit from unearned income gained through dropouts and nonstarts.[15] In a "mixed economy" of publicly and privately owned schools, private home study schools have provided instruction for millions of students. They claim the right to be judged by their performance, not by their financial position.

However, CERP cannot overlook the importance of the profit motive in determining such important issues as public acceptance of the correspondence method, the percentage of operating revenue that can be spent on instruction, and the attention a school can and will pay to the problems of the individual student. Profit making per se need not be bad, but it can create conditions which produce undesirable results.

Statistical Comparison

CERP has singled out the universities and the private home study schools for special consideration. Philosophical disputes and conflicting goals make the financial operation of these two types of suppliers more complex than those of the other eight types. CERP examined these complexities in detail because of their influence on other problems facing all correspondence suppliers.

Table 3–1 gives the statistical base for some of the CERP observations. Only limited information was available as many institutions are reticent about details of their financial operation. Nevertheless, CERP attempts to give an approximation of the percentage distribution of expenditures by private home study schools and university correspondence departments. USAFI makes available the details of its financial operation, and these statistics are included to give a basis for comparison. CERP surveyed only the better schools and programs in order to avoid including the degree-mill extremes that might distort the normal range of statistics.

MAINTAINING A QUALITY STAFF

Teaching by correspondence requires highly specialized skills. Certain characteristics of the method—particularly the distance between the student and his instructor—make special demands on correspondence staff. Consequently a skilled staff is of critical importance, a fact recognized by correspondence directors. Private home study school directors ranked the need for cap-

TABLE 3-1

*Percentage distribution of budget expenditure**

ITEMS OF EXPENDITURE	COLLEGE AND UNIVERSITY			PRIVATE HOME STUDY SCHOOLS			USAFI
	Medium-sized programs		Large programs	Medium-sized schools		Nonprofit schools	Fiscal year 1965
	Range, %	Mean, %	Range, %	Range, %	Mean, %	Range, %	%
Operating cost (total)	32.5–42.8	39.5	35.1–51.0	29.1–38.8	33.7	41.1–na†	21.0
Administrative and clerical (including wages)	21.0–27.0	26.1	21.6–32.0	nbd‡	....	17.3–na	18.0
Facilities (plant, office supplies, non-promotional mail)	11.5–15.8	13.4	13.5–19.0	nbd	....	23.8–na	3.0
Instructional cost (total)	49.9–66.0	56.9	43.0–52.2	17.1–28.3	22.8	36.0–51.8	79.0§
Course services (preparing, correcting, grading, testing)	46.9–62.0	53.6	40.0–48.0	12.0–22.3	17.4	nbd	nbd
Course development and revision	3.0–4.0	3.3	3.0–4.2	5.1–6.0	5.4	nbd	nbd

Promotional cost (total)	1.0–5.1	3.4	3.5–4.2	30.6–58.9	43.5	7.1–50.0	0
Advertising and promotion (including promotional mail)	1.0–5.1	3.4	3.5–4.2	15.6–30.0	21.2	nbd	0
Sales representatives (salaries and expenses)	0	0	0	15.0–28.9	22.3	nbd	0

* CERP survey information taken from a selective survey of universities, private home study schools, and USAFI. Survey samples are limited and indicate general patterns, not statistically accurate or exhaustive results.

† na = not available.

‡ nbd = not broken down.

§ = This figure includes 8 percent for USAFI testing program, 3 percent for participating college program, and 1 percent for dependents' schools program.

able personnel as their third most serious problem (ranked ahead of financial problems!). University correspondence directors included "obtaining competent and enthusiastic instructors" and "professionalism of correspondence administrators and staff members" among their most pressing needs.

Staff Qualities Needed

The correspondence *administrator* needs special qualities of foresight. He must predict the behavior of a group of students he never sees and probably knows little about. He must plan courses and specify course objectives—activities to be discussed at length in Chapter 4—for a heterogeneous and geographically diffuse group. He must be able to run his program on a tight budget and be good at devising alternative solutions when the best appears to be too expensive. He may have to develop considerable bargaining skill to convince his superiors of the value of correspondence programs and to persuade competent teachers to devote some of their time to correspondence instruction. Finally, the administrator must have ingenuity to overcome any obstacles that might prevent his program from achieving the objectives set for it by the institution.

The *course writer* must be particularly sensitive to his special task. In correspondence instruction, the burden of the actual teaching function rests squarely on the written word. The writer must be able to prepare clear and authoritative texts and syllabi; ambiguity, poor exposition, or inaccurate material can be disastrous when there is no teacher present to modify the written text. The expert correspondence course writer can predict student questions and answer them in the text. As a prerequisite in some programs, course writers may be required to have passed certificate qualifications (for which the course is being prepared), or to have a recognized academic degree in the discipline. Too rarely, however, are course writers expected to have experience in correspondence instruction or be experts in the particular skills needed to produce a quality course.

The correspondence *instructor* must be as knowledgeable as a resident instructor. But he must also be able to evaluate a student's progress from a limited written response and determine what additional help the student may need. Paul Woodring gave the following criteria for a good correspondence instructor in a CERP staff paper:

> If correspondence courses are to stimulate creativity, it is obvious that the teachers of such courses must be carefully selected. In addition to being better informed and more highly educated than the students they must be at least as intelligent, perceptive, and capable of creativity as the brightest of their students. And, because some of the students are likely to be very bright indeed, it is essential that the teachers be of very superior intellect—it takes brains to spot a brain. The papers submitted by correspondence students should be read by highly qualified teachers, not by sub-professional assistants.

The correspondence course *grader* cannot be defined by any collective set of characteristics. For some programs, computers may be used to grade simple responses. In others, a grader may need only to be able to use a simple grid to check off responses. Some suppliers actually specify that they prefer to use older women or people with little training because they are less likely to become bored with grid or check-off grading. However, some suppliers do attempt to elicit more complex responses from their students. In a CERP survey on teaching methods, 68.4 percent of the suppliers responding claim to use some kind of subjective problems or tests as one of their most important teaching devices.[16] Although CERP experience indicates that this figure is an exaggeration, a skilled and sensitive grader is needed whenever subjective responses must be graded. When objective grading can be handled by untrained individuals, such characteristics as having taken the course, military rank, or salary demands may be used to determine which candidate will get the job.

Problems in Obtaining and Holding Staff

One of the major difficulties in obtaining qualified personnel for correspondence instruction programs is simply that such personnel do not exist. Courses preparing prospective teachers in the correspondence method are sorely lacking. In fact, most students complete teacher training without ever having studied the correspondence method of instruction. In addition, correspondence instruction is only beginning to gain importance in continuing education for practicing teachers. As a result, many teachers have never used correspondence instruction at all.

Educators in general have had little contact with correspondence instruction and often display considerable ignorance about what it is and how it operates. A CERP survey of educators produced such responses as "I have had no contact with correspondence instruction" or "For my own part, I am completely uninterested in this at all." When one considers that a limited supply of teachers must be spread among the various instructional methods, this ignorance puts correspondence instruction at a considerable disadvantage.

Deans and department heads, jealous of the time of their instructors, are often unwilling to cooperate with the correspondence director who is seeking to recruit new members for his staff.

Even apart from the quality of adult education, deans and department heads prefer to have their faculty do research in their spare time rather than teach additional courses, so that on principle their cooperation with the general-extension division is reluctant and partial.[17]

As long as correspondence instruction is held in such low esteem, correspondence directors will find it difficult to get a fair share of the limited teacher supply.

Inadequate pay also makes teachers reluctant to undertake correspondence instruction. For example, in the early years of correspondence instruction development, university correspondence departments rarely paid authors for course syllabi. Subsequent instructional fees from the course were expected to pay them for their time and effort. Now authors commonly receive an honorarium for writing a course in addition to instructional fees they may earn later. This honorarium may be merely a token $50 for a three-credit course or as high as $500 for a particularly difficult syllabus. Course writers in the military or other training organizations typically operate on a flat salaried basis.

Instructional payments are not much more advantageous. Universities pay a flat fee of from $0.70 to $2.60 per student lesson. Often there is a bonus for rapid work. Instructors' fees in other supplier groups are also likely to be modest. Graders' fees tend to be the lowest of all as qualifications are lowest and the work is often the most trivial.

Lack of prestige presents another important block that correspondence directors must overcome if they are to lure more and better administrators and teachers. Even the impressive title of "director" may carry little academic prestige when attached to correspondence instruction. There is no existing hierarchy among correspondence instructors, and as a group they stand collectively outside the ranks of academia. A low salary can frequently be compensated by a little prestige, but when both adequate pay and prestige are lacking in a job it is unlikely to seem very attractive. Perhaps because these obstacles eliminate the indifferent, correspondence staffs often turn out to be extremely dedicated to their task. They stay in their jobs because they feel they have a mission to accomplish: to give an equal opportunity to those who can best be served by correspondence instruction. Only recently, with a few attempts at raising salaries and improving the image of correspondence departments, have professional educators attempted to establish correspondence instruction on the same financial and prestige basis as the more traditional instruction methods. The current trend toward professionalism must be encouraged if correspondence instruction is to continue to fill its personnel needs in a competitive market.

DEFINING THE CORRESPONDENCE STUDENT

One of the major problems facing the supplier of correspondence instruction is identifying the characteristics of his student body. A CERP staff paper by Peter H. Rossi and John W. C. Johnstone of the National Opinion Research Center (NORC) attempts to define the correspondence student by his average or collective characteristics. Although this profile says little about the individual student, it does give a working outline of characteristics of the correspondence student body.

Table 3–2 presents the sex, age, years of formal education, and median family income of the average correspondence student. Results are based on a random survey taken in nearly twelve thousand different households in the United States.

TABLE 3-2

Profile of the typical adult student

STUDENT CHARACTERISTIC	CORRESPONDENCE STUDENTS	ALL STUDENTS	SURVEY SAMPLE
Sex			
Male	75%	50%	47%
Female	25%	50%	53%
Age, years			
Median	33.2	36.5	42.8
Base	344	4,678	23,677
Years of formal education			
Median	12.2	12.2	11.5
Base	345	4,681	23,299
Family income			
Median	$5,880	$6,600	$5,410
Base	344	4,637	23,123

Figures are given for the following: those participating specifically in correspondence instruction (correspondence students); all those participating in any kind of study program, including correspondence study (all students); and all those interviewed, both students and nonstudents (survey sample).

The predominance of male over female students in correspondence instruction presents a striking statistic.

The age characteristic may be deceiving. The Rossi and Johnstone profile covers only adult learners, thus eliminating the largest student group (those five to twenty-one years old). In addition, the survey was made in homes, bypassing the large group of students in the military. As noted in Chapter 1, military personnel make up over 60 percent of those enrolled in correspondence instruction in this country. Nevertheless it is interesting to note that the average correspondence student from the survey group is 3.2 years younger than the average adult student and 9.6 years younger than the average person interviewed. Interest in correspondence instruction seems to wane as the student gets older.

The median number of years of formal education of the adult correspondence student, 12.2 years, or slightly better than a high school degree, equaled the median number of years of formal education of all students in the survey. Those correspondence students with between nine and fifteen years of formal education relied much more heavily on correspondence instruction than did those with less than nine or more than fifteen years. Those who reached their senior year in college or beyond and those who dropped out in their freshman year of high school or before generally do not use correspondence instruction.

Although the median annual income of the average correspondence student is $470 higher than that of the average person interviewed, it is also $720 lower than that of the average adult learner. This may be explained in part by the increase in earning power of those motivated to continue learning past their initial formal schooling over those who do not. The 3.2 year age difference may, in turn, be partially responsible for the younger correspondence students' earning less than the other adult learners. Use of correspondence instruction is clearly highest among individuals in the $4,000 to $5,999 income bracket, indicating that correspondence instruction has earned the reputation of being a poor man's school.

Table 3-3 shows that over one-third of those already in the labor force and using correspondence instruction classify themselves as craftsmen or foremen. Professional and technical workers make up the other large occupational concentration,

TABLE 3-3

Occupational distribution of adult students in the labor force

OCCUPATION	CORRESPONDENCE STUDENTS	ALL STUDENTS	SURVEY SAMPLE
Craftsmen and foremen	36%	18%	16%
Professional and technical workers	18%	23%	12%
Managers, officials, and proprietors	11%	12%	11%
Clerical and office workers	10%	15%	13%
Operatives	10%	10%	17%
Other	15%	22%	31%
Base	295	3,321	14,265

although they account for only half as many correspondence students as the foremen and craftsmen. Together these two groups constitute more than 50 percent of the workers who study by correspondence. CERP infers from these statistics that correspondence instruction can be used with particular success in these occupational areas.

Table 3–4 shows that correspondence instruction is most widely used in rural areas and urban populations of low density. The survey indicates that 44 percent of adult correspondence students live in areas of under fifty thousand; only 29 percent of all adult learners live in similar areas. This statistic strongly supports the suggestion that correspondence instruction is useful to those geographically isolated from resident learning centers.

TABLE 3-4

Adult student population distribution

AREA	CORRESPONDENCE STUDENTS	ALL STUDENTS	SURVEY SAMPLE
Large city (over 2 million)	16%	25%	23%
Medium-sized city (50,000–2 million)	40%	45%	40%
Small city (10,000–50,000)	22%	13%	14%
Rural area or small town (under 10,000)	22%	16%	23%
Base	345	4,710	23,840

Note: The Rossi and Johnstone profile makes no provision for disparities among the students, but supplier groups recognize that their students sometimes differ significantly from the median. The University of California correspondence department reports that only 54 percent of its students under the age of thirty-five are male, and beyond that age female students hold the majority. The International Correspondence Schools (ICS) found that over 91 percent of their 1963 student body were men; most of the enrollees at the Weaver Airline Personnel School were women.

The median correspondence student has a high school degree; yet 96 percent of the estimated 130,000 students at American School have not graduated from high school, while 35 percent of the University of California correspondence students have college degrees. Age groups also vary greatly from the median: military personnel taking correspondence instruction, through either the Armed Forces or the USAFI, are typically under twenty-one years of age, while seminary and Bible institute students are usually between thirty and forty-five years old.

Although the Rossi and Johnstone profile gives an interesting description of the typical student, each supplier must look carefully at the characteristics of his own students if he is to handle their particular problems successfully.

Student Motivation

Because of the independent nature of correspondence study, correspondence students who finish their courses are typically more highly motivated than students using other study methods. Yet private home study schools rank student motivation as their most severe problem, and university correspondence directors, USAFI, and military correspondence administrators also indicate that motivating students is one of their most serious and difficult tasks.

There are basically two kinds of motivating stimuli: one motivates the student to satisfy a personal desire for knowledge; the other responds to a demand for some kind of instruction leading to career advancement. Rossi and Johnstone indicate in their survey that the typical student takes correspondence instruction to achieve career advancement rather than personal goals.

Students motivated by specific goals of advancement may be more likely to endure the difficulties of a study program. The student seeking academic credit will often be motivated by the idea of receiving an academic degree and subsequently obtaining a good job. Advancement in business or industry may depend directly on success in company-sponsored correspondence programs. Both job prestige and salary increases help motivate workers in such programs. Certain jobs are closed to anyone not bearing certification or a license. Correspondence instruction leading to such qualifications has high built-in motivation; so do correspondence programs in the Armed Forces and in federal government agencies leading to promotion and retirement pension credit.

Student Admissions Policies

Who should be allowed to take a correspondence course? Some argue that anyone who is motivated to study by correspondence may profit and should be given the opportunity to do so. Others argue that correspondence programs should be selective and try to screen out potential dropouts and failures at the start.

Specifying students who should take a course is an important supplier problem. For business and industry, the federal government, professional and trade organizations, the Armed Forces, and labor unions, however, the problem is minimal. They are all trying to train personnel, and their main concern is to be sure that the students they specify for correspondence instruction are capable of learning by that method. Admission practices are typically permissive. Approval of the commanding officer is the usual criterion for student selection in the Armed Forces. Some business correspondence programs allow employees to take even advanced engineering courses on the basis of field experience without requiring any previous academic qualifications. One professional association's correspondence administrator reports that his program sets course prerequisites, "However, we do not insist that they be met if the member is determined to enroll in the course."

Religious organizations and USAFI also have fairly permissive admissions policies. USAFI does establish course prerequisites and expects students to meet them before enrolling. As most of the groups mentioned so far offer their courses free or at a nominal charge, students are unlikely to complain of being lured into an unsatisfactory program. In addition, the organization expects to benefit from the improved performance of the student. If the organization is happy with the results it achieves, it is unlikely to change to a more rigorous screening process without some strong impetus.

Correspondence departments in universities are generally the most restrictive in their admissions policy. If the enrollee is seeking degree credit, he may be asked to meet requirements as rigorous as those for resident students. Correspondence directors frequently demand transcripts of previous academic experience and recommendations from previous administrators for those who transfer from another institution or who are in academic difficulty. When the student is a high school graduate not seeking degree credit, restrictions are often waived. However, department catalogs frequently warn the student that he is expected to have certain prior knowledge as indicated by course prerequisites.

The admissions policies of private home study schools are generally wide open. These schools tend to place considerable confidence in the student's ability to know what is best for himself. As the late Albert Dorne, former president of Famous Artists and Writers Schools, put it: "When a person pays hard-earned money for one of our courses, he means business and we are obligated to take him seriously."[18] Most schools have some kind of screening process to avoid obvious misregistrations, but the rejection rate is admittedly low. The salesman also can use his discretion to dissuade a prospective student who is unqualified, but since the salesman is usually paid on a commission basis, he is unlikely to pass up a sale at his own expense. For legal reasons, however, he must take particular precautions in enrolling minors.

Postadmission Guidance

The distance between supplier and student poses a serious obstacle to adequate student guidance. None of the supplier groups can provide as complete and readily available guidance as a resident institution. Yet many correspondence programs try to make guidance counseling available to their students.

The Armed Forces have the closest geographical contact with their students. Educational officers on military bases help students with their instructional problems. USAFI offers to answer any student questions mailed to the USAFI center. Universities often extend similar offers to give attention to student problems mailed to the correspondence center.

Students taking correspondence courses through business or industry, religious organizations, labor unions, or associations can frequently get answers to their questions from the appropriate source within the organization. Frequently the person who enrolled them in the course is also responsible for watching their progress. This, however, is not the case in most private home study schools. The salesman is rarely qualified to give professional counseling or educational advice to the student. Some schools respond to student queries with promotional literature instead of personal answers.

The student who does not receive adequate counseling when he runs into difficulty cannot be expected to complete the course. His problem may be motivational or intellectual, but he deserves the attention of a trained counselor. As Dr. B. LaMar Johnson, nationally prominent junior college authority, observed: "It is difficult to defend the admission of all comers unless we provide offerings and counseling adapted to the requirements of our clientele."[19]

Course Completion

CERP pointed out earlier that some private home study and university correspondence programs depend on student nonstarts and dropouts for their financial livelihood. Yet most correspondence suppliers are deeply concerned about how to encourage higher completion rates in their programs. The following discussion of course completion problems will be based upon these strict definitions:

> *nonstart:* a student who registers for a course by correspondence, pays all or part of the tuition fee, and receives his packet of materials but never submits a single lesson.
>
> *dropout:* a student who registers for a course by correspondence, pays all or part of the tuition fee, submits one or more lessons but discontinues his participation in the course before completing it.

The nonstart problem is quite a serious one. The supplier interested in training a student through correspondence instruction fails totally with the nonstart.

The supplier of education who enrolls a nonstart may shrug it off, claiming to have offered the opportunity. Frequently, a high percentage of nonstarts will give the supplying institution reason to reexamine its enrollment and screening procedures.

Many private home study schools are concerned with their nonstart problem. But as the nonstart who has paid a large part of his tuition generally brings a higher profit, many suppliers are happy to reap the quick windfall. When tuition refunds are demanded or materials are sent before the student has paid for them, financial self-interest demands some supplier action.

Table 3–5 gives the range of nonstarts in a limited sample of the various kinds of suppliers. Statistics are taken from a CERP survey of suppliers and are meant to form approximate limits. Upper extremes are generally excluded.

A nonstart is easy to identify: he never submits his first lesson. The dropout is not so easy to distinguish because each supplier has his own method of determining just when a course is completed. Some insist that a course is completed only when a final examination is successfully passed. Others indicate that a course may be completed after a certain percentage of the course lessons have been submitted. Some correspondence suppliers give separate statistics for course graduates and course completions. Their percentage of graduates indicates the number of students who have submitted all course work and thereby graduated. Their percentage of course completions (which generally excludes nonstarts but includes statistics for all graduates) actually indicates the percentage of lessons submitted out of

TABLE 3-5

Percentage of student nonstarts

SUPPLIER	RANGE, %
Armed Forces	0–30
Business and industry	5–20
Federal government (FAA)	20
Private home study schools	0–30
State governments	10–20
Universities	0–30
USAFI	50

the total number required of all students enrolled. Thus course completion statistics can be extremely deceptive.

Course completion statistics are doubly misleading if one attempts to generalize from them. A student may drop out because the work is too difficult or because he does not have sufficient motivation to keep up with the work. But he may also stop submitting lessons because he has satisfied personal goals before the completion of the course. According to Gayle B. Childs:

> In regard to completion rates, it must be borne in mind that a completion rate of 100 per cent will never be attained in correspondence study courses. Many people enroll in such courses with no intention of completing the work. For example, some students, who are preparing to enter college, register for mathematics as a refresher course before taking entrance examinations. These students drop when they feel they have acquired what they need to know. Some institutions concerned with mental health use correspondence courses for occupational therapy. Registrants from these institutions rarely finish the courses for which they are enrolled. Again, not all high schools require the completion of a correspondence course before granting credit. . . . In all of the above cases, the purpose for which the pupil enrolled was accomplished even though the registration is recorded at the correspondence center as not having been completed. Completion percentages are therefore deceptively low.[20]

Some private home study schools report that as many as 70 percent of their students fail to complete courses for which they are enrolled. Correspondence programs in business and industry report that as few as 10 percent actually complete certain courses. University correspondence directors indicate that approximately 27 percent of the students submit at least one lesson but drop out before finishing.

Although these statistics may contain many dropouts who are perfectly satisfied with their correspondence instruction experience, few suppliers are so naive as to overlook the need to encourage course completion. Suppliers rely on motivational techniques to stimulate the student to continue. Private home study schools, the Armed Forces, business and industry, and federal agencies all use letters to encourage the delinquent student to catch up. Business and industry and federal agencies frequently grant released time for study to those having difficulty with continuing their studies while at work. Private home study schools often send salesmen around to call and follow up with free gifts and a renewed flow of promotional literature. The Armed Forces rely on notification through the mail and occasional encouragement from educational officers, while the state governments in some instances expect the correspondence instructors to make contact with dropouts.

One fairly common means of preventing dropouts is to use complimentary grading to encourage poor students. The belief is that a student will not drop out if he is doing well. Consequently, course standards may be partially determined by the supplier's estimate of the student's need for praise.

> Grading is one tool that can be used in helping the student build a positive image of himself. Grading high is more likely to encourage the student, to make him want to live up to the high opinion that the instructor has of him. Low grading does not make the student work harder. Adult students, especially those in a correspondence course, enroll because they want to learn, probably because they have the desire to do something to improve themselves. To grade low focuses attention on the grade instead of on the learning process, discourages the student, and in some cases causes him to give up.[21]

The most successful method of encouraging course completion seems to be by linking advancement directly to course results. When promotions or pay raises depend upon course completion, dropouts and nonstarts are greatly reduced. Other achievement incentives, such as posting a list of course graduates or granting special certificates and diplomas, also prove effective.

In order to solve his particular noncompletion problems, each supplier must determine why his students are nonstarts or dropouts. Then he can best decide whether faulty enrollment procedure, lack of adequate guidance, or discouragement caused the discontinuation or whether the student dropped out because he had already satisfied his own goals. Only at that point will the supplier be able to make meaningful changes toward a higher percentage of course completions. CERP recognizes that dropouts and nonstarts now form an integral part of the budget calculations of many university correspondence programs and actually provide the margin of profit for many private home study schools. Nevertheless, CERP is concerned that acceptance of the dropout and nonstart rate may sometimes lessen supplier efforts to encourage students to complete course objectives.

GAINING ACCEPTANCE OF
CORRESPONDENCE INSTRUCTION

Suppliers recognize that improving the image of the correspondence instruction method is one of their most pressing tasks. For despite the growth of the method and the services it extends to nearly three million students annually, correspondence instruction has not succeeded in convincing the skeptics or creating a favorable public image for itself. This general lack of acceptance impedes the correspondence director in his search for (1) financial support, (2) qualified staff, (3) higher enrollment, and (4) academic credit for correspondence courses.

Lack of acceptance of the method by businessmen, educational administrators, and government officials restricts the funds available for correspondence programs. The poor image correspondence instruction has among teachers makes it difficult for the correspondence administrator to staff his program. Lack of confidence in the correspondence method and fear of fraudulent programs may keep students away from correspondence programs. Finally, refusal to accept credit earned through correspondence instruction hurts the supplier, the teacher, and the student. The method cannot achieve its instructional potential so long as a poor image restricts its operation.

Attitudes of the Opinion Makers

CERP conducted a survey among a highly selective group of outstanding public figures and influential citizens from various occupations to determine their attitudes toward correspondence instruction. The more than 800 responses were carefully analyzed to determine the image of correspondence instruction held by these opinion makers.

Covering letters from respondents provided the survey's first conclusion: many opinion makers have given little thought to correspondence instruction. They expressed their ignorance about its operation by such typical comments as "I don't know much about correspondence instruction, but here are my quick, off-the-cuff impressions." This fairly widespread ignorance of the method among the opinion makers indicates that the survey responses should be read as the candid opinions of influential people, not as the considered deliberations of experts.

This ignorance is a problem of considerable importance. Influential people may be unwilling to back the use of a method with which they have had little contact; they are certainly unlikely to suggest its use or think of it at all when called upon to solve a particular instructional problem.

CERP asked the opinion makers to compare correspondence instruction as a method with four other instructional methods. In all categories, they expressed their personal opinion that correspondence instruction is not as good as the other four methods. (See Appendix A for survey methodology.) The results are shown in Figure 3–1.

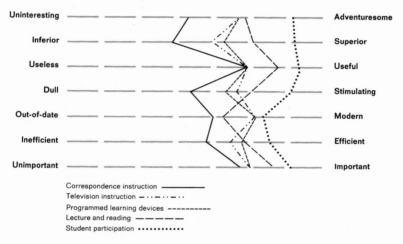

Figure 3–1 Opinion makers' ratings of several instructional media and methods.

Attitudes of the Educators

In analyzing the opinion makers' survey, CERP noticed that the educators in the group consistently gave lower ratings to correspondence instruction than did the opinion makers in general. It should be pointed out, however, that educators gave lower appraisals of all the methods considered except the traditional lecture and tutorial methods. Wayland J. Chase predicted this kind of conservative behavior on the part of academics who refused to accept correspondence instruction:

> Doubtless the conservatism of scholars has been one cause of their scepticism, for the first reaction of many men to the new is always one of fear and suspicion, and apprehension of the untried might be expected naturally of those whose life task is the inculcation of the lessons of experience.[22]

Educators play a particularly important role in determining the acceptance of any educational method. As Grant Venn observed: "Correspondence work . . . would become more valued in the public mind if [it] were more valued by the 'fashion makers' in this nation's colleges and universities."[23] As colleges and universities sit on the top of the educational ladder, they lend prestige to whatever they support. In the section above on obtaining qualified staff, CERP reported that educators were generally uninformed about correspondence instruction. Books and articles on education frequently fail to mention correspondence instruction at all. This ignorance perhaps accounts for some of the educators' impression that the method is inferior. Figure 3-2 compares the views of the educators with the views of the other opinion makers on both the potential of the method and the quality of actual instruction in the United States today.

The narrow interpretation of the university function—as a center for research and education of the elite—naturally influences the opinion of educators who accept it. If they feel that extension programs threaten the quality of university instruction, they are not likely to rate correspondence instruction very highly. Thus university politics may militate against educators having a high opinion of the correspondence method.

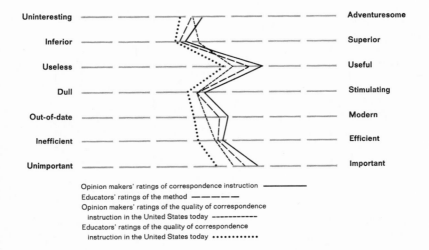

Uninteresting ————————————————————— Adventuresome
Inferior ————————————————————— Superior
Useless ————————————————————— Useful
Dull ————————————————————— Stimulating
Out-of-date ————————————————————— Modern
Inefficient ————————————————————— Efficient
Unimportant ————————————————————— Important

Opinion makers' ratings of correspondence instruction ————————
Educators' ratings of the method ——————
Opinion makers' ratings of the quality of correspondence
   instruction in the United States today ——————————
Educators' ratings of the quality of correspondence
   instruction in the United States today ••••••••••••

Figure 3–2   Ratings by opinion makers, as a group, and educators of the correspondence instructional method and of the quality of correspondence instruction in the United States today.

As shown in Figure 3–3, educators and opinion makers generally agree on the best uses for correspondence instruction. Continuing education, retraining, and vocational study receive the strongest recommendations. Most of the respondents also feel strongly that correspondence instruction should be used in conjunction with other instructional methods. The main discrepancy arises over the educators' lower appraisal of the correspondence method for graduate university education.

Attitudes of the Professions

While educators and opinion makers express somewhat unenthusiastic views of correspondence instruction, some potential users reject the method outright. Claiming either that it is unsuitable to their particular needs or that the method is simply

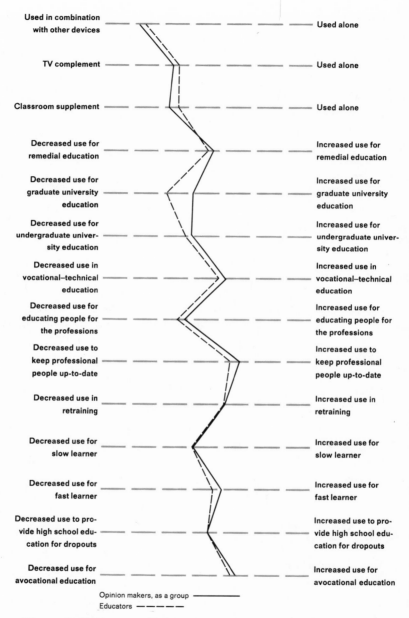

Used in combination with other devices		Used alone
TV complement		Used alone
Classroom supplement		Used alone
Decreased use for remedial education		Increased use for remedial education
Decreased use for graduate university education		Increased use for graduate university education
Decreased use for undergraduate university education		Increased use for undergraduate university education
Decreased use in vocational–technical education		Increased use in vocational–technical education
Decreased use for educating people for the professions		Increased use for educating people for the professions
Decreased use to keep professional people up-to-date		Increased use to keep professional people up-to-date
Decreased use in retraining		Increased use in retraining
Decreased use for slow learner		Increased use for slow learner
Decreased use for fast learner		Increased use for fast learner
Decreased use to provide high school education for dropouts		Increased use to provide high school education for dropouts
Decreased use for avocational education		Increased use for avocational education

Opinion makers, as a group ——————
Educators — — — — —

Figure 3–3 Ratings by opinion makers, as a group, and by educators of the best uses for correspondence instruction.

inferior, certain groups refuse to allow any credit for study through correspondence.

REJECTION DE JURE   The American Bar Association through its Section of Legal Education and Admissions to the Bar flatly states: "The American Bar Association expressly disapproves of correspondence law courses as a means of preparation for bar examinations and for practice."[24] Only two states permit a student to take bar examinations with a law degree earned through correspondence courses.

REJECTION DE FACTO   Associations representing medicine, dentistry, and nursing take no formal position against correspondence instruction. Yet letters to CERP from education officials in the American Medical Association, the American Dental Association, and the National League for Nursing indicate that they are unaware of any use of correspondence instruction leading to entry into these three professions.

LIMITED ACCEPTANCE   Some groups recognize the value of correspondence instruction but approve of it only when combined with other instructional methods. The American Council on Pharmaceutical Education allows students to earn some of the credits toward a degree in pharmacy through correspondence instruction; but correspondence credit is not accepted in any of the laboratory sciences or pharmacy courses, only in the general subjects needed for graduation. Colleges generally permit prospective teachers to take from one-fourth to one-third of their undergraduate program through correspondence. Some correspondence courses leading to ordainment are offered by various seminaries.

ACCEPTANCE   Many certified public accountants receive their only formal training through correspondence, and many more have used correspondence instruction to review for the Uniform CPA Examination. In most states, if not in all, an engineering student may prepare himself for the Engineer-in-Training Examination by correspondence instruction or any means available. The Armed Forces are also very liberal in their acceptance of correspondence credits toward promotion.

CREDIT AND ACCREDITATION

Suppliers who offer correspondence instruction for their own training needs obviously will accept a student's qualifications earned through correspondence. But most students have to carry their credentials to a prospective employer in the form of a degree or training credit earned elsewhere. Before the student can be sure his hours spent in correspondence study will be recognized, correspondence suppliers must convince the academic community and potential employers of the validity of the method.

Some colleges and universities do not allow any credit toward a degree to be earned through correspondence instruction. A CERP survey of forty-four institutions which do accept credit earned through correspondence instruction shows that exactly one-half of them allow a student to take 25 percent of his degree credit through correspondence courses; two others allow only 12 percent by correspondence, while three others accept up to 50 percent. Some departments reject correspondence course credit even when the parent university policy is permissive. Interestingly enough, some institutions which place severe restrictions on the amount of correspondence credit they will accept have been in the position of accepting such credits earned by students transferring from other institutions simply because transcripts frequently do not indicate how credits are earned.

Responses of individual educators to a CERP questionnaire asking how many credit hours of a 120 credit hour baccalaureate degree they would allow to be taken by correspondence indicated that:

10 percent would permit	more than 30 credits
30 percent would permit	from 16 to 30 credits
30 percent would permit	15 credits or fewer

The Office of Education of the U. S. Department of Health, Education, and Welfare states categorically: "Degrees for work done wholly by correspondence are not granted or recognized by accredited colleges and universities or accepted by examining boards of the different professions in the several states."[25]

But even the granting of university credit is not always satisfactory. Although the public is generally confident of the quality of work done at a resident institution, many feel that it is too difficult to judge the quality of a correspondence course. The public desire for some common evaluation of correspondence courses and the need to tell before enrolling which courses will be acceptable to employers or to academic institutions led to the practice of accreditation in correspondence instruction.

William K. Selden, former executive director of the National Commission on Accrediting, gives a clear definition of the term: "Accrediting is the process whereby an organization or agency recognizes a college or university or a program of study as having met certain predetermined qualifications or standards."[26] Accreditation has come to serve several different functions, including the following:

1. Certifying that the institution or program has met certain established standards

2. Indicating to foundations or government grant-giving agencies which programs meet requirements for their support

3. Creating a goal for self-improvement of weaker programs and stimulating a general raising of standards among educational institutions

4. Standardizing credits and establishing a basis for credit transfer

5. Providing a basis for professional certification, licensure, or general preparation, and upgrading courses offering such preparation

6. Helping programs resist undesirable pressures to lower standards for nonacademic reasons

THE MECHANISM OF ACCREDITATION   For the most part, accreditation is voluntary. Government research agencies, companies offering tuition refunds, or colleges examining a student's high school record may all stipulate that only courses taken through accredited programs are acceptable, and programs competing for students may feel at a disadvantage if they cannot claim accreditation. However, no external pressure beyond this compels a correspondence program to seek accreditation.

There are two basic forms of accreditation: general accreditation is performed by some national or regional body and judges the qualifications of the supplying institution; specific accreditation is granted by business, professional, or state or federal government units and applies only to specific programs acceptable to those organizations on a credit basis. Because accrediting is a voluntary practice, its value depends on the recognition the accrediting agency can win.

Any group or agency can perform an accrediting function if those it purports to represent are willing to recognize it.

Early in this century, a number of accrediting agencies arose. However, the need for uniform standards led to the consolidation of many of them. In 1949 the colleges and universities founded the National Commission on Accrediting (NCA).

> The Commission was "designated by consent of its members [colleges and universities] to speak and act for them with respect to policies and procedures of accrediting agencies whose operations directly affect the administration or programs of institutions of higher education."[27]

The NCA does not itself perform an accrediting function; however, it authorizes six regional associations to perform general accrediting tasks and twenty-five professional organizations to grant specific accreditation.

The need for private home study schools to unite and provide some kind of guarantee to the public of the quality of their instructional offerings was spotted by Noffsinger in 1926.

> The reputable schools for their own sake must take the initiative in bringing the arm of the law against the diploma mill. Theirs is primarily a moral responsibility. They also have a professional obligation. Pedagogically education by correspondence is almost terra incognita. . . .
>
> Joint effort by the reputable and well-established schools will not only create public confidence in the correspondence school but lay a science of education by correspondence. Out of such effort certain standards of practice will develop, ethically and educationally. Correctives to certain defects in the best schools will be worked out naturally.[28]

Later that same year, spurred on by Noffsinger's words, some of the more responsible private correspondence suppliers founded the National Home Study Council with twelve charter members. The NHSC provides accreditation to private home study schools. The Association of Home Study Schools (AHSS), composed mostly of smaller private home study schools, serves as a trade association and not as an accrediting agency; it publishes a list of approved member schools.

The U. S. Commissioner of Education is legally empowered to recognize accrediting organizations. Under his authority, the Office of Education has recognized the six regional and twenty-five professional accrediting bodies comprising the NCA, the New York State Board of Regents (for higher education in New York State), and the NHSC's Accrediting Commission. It is important to note that the NCA accrediting bodies and the Board of Regents accredit instructional institutions; correspondence programs within these institutions automatically receive the approval granted to the parent body. The NHSC is the only recognized group set up specifically to perform an accrediting function for correspondence instruction programs.

Despite their many differences, these accrediting agencies generally follow similar patterns of procedure involving five basic steps:

1. Standards are established; having evolved from cooperative efforts of institutions, they are usually codified by the accrediting agency.

2. The institution or unit to be accredited usually prepares a self-evaluation study that measures its performance in terms of established standards or qualifications.

3. A team selected by the accrediting agency visits the institution or unit to judge firsthand whether the institution meets the standards.

4. Following the visit, if the accrediting agency is satisfied that the standards have been met, the institution or unit is listed in an official publication with other similarly approved institutions or units.

5. There are usually periodic reevaluations of the institution or unit to ascertain that standards continue to be met.

The recognized accrediting bodies insist on compliance with their established standards. The NHSC lists eight different criteria which must be satisfied for accreditation; these effectively indicate the areas of concern of the accrediting agency:

1. Competent faculty

2. Educationally sound and up-to-date courses

3. Careful screening of students for admission

4. Satisfactory educational services

5. Demonstrated ample student success and satisfaction

6. Reasonable tuition charges

7. Truthful advertisement of courses

8. Financial capability of giving high-quality service

There is one other significant accrediting agency that should be mentioned. In 1945, the American Council on Education (ACE) established the Commission on Accreditation of Service Experiences (CASE) to evaluate and make credit recommendations for USAFI courses. CASE, a private and civilian organization, advises schools, colleges, and businesses on the value of a serviceman's USAFI instruction and to this end assists in standardizing USAFI grading and examination procedures. CASE also offers its services to military personnel who have not taken USAFI courses:

> If an individual has acquired competence in a subject through other ways than study of a USAFI course, and can demonstrate satisfactory achievement [on USAFI tests,] . . . the Commission recommends that the same amount of credit be granted as though the student had studied the USAFI course.[29]

Two testing services, although not actually accrediting bodies, perform the similar function of validating an individual's academic experience. The General Educational Development (GED) testing service offers a high school equivalency certification to those who have not been able to complete resident high school requirements. In all but two of the fifty states and in the District of Columbia, the Canal Zone, Guam, Puerto Rico, and Samoa, any adult citizen, whether military or civilian, may earn an equivalency certificate through passing the GED examinations. "The equivalency certificates are widely accepted in lieu of high school diplomas," a CASE bulletin reads. "Business, industry, civil service commissions, and state and local boards of licensing examiners recognize them as meeting the requirement of high school graduation in job eligibility and promotions."[30] However, the GED service makes no provision for validating achievement in a particular subject; it rates only the individual's total educational experience.

The College Entrance Examination Board (CEEB) working through its Council on College-Level Examinations has constructed a series of general and subject examinations to validate students' educational experiences gained outside the formal system such as through home study or on-the-job training. In 1967 the examinations became available nationally to unaffiliated students through fifty-one examining centers. Not only have about forty colleges agreed to grant credit based on examination results, but these tests also provide a measuring stick by which a college or employer can evaluate and compare the learning experiences of students coming from different institutions. New York State's Board of Regents established its similar College Proficiency Examination Program "in an effort to open more widely the educational opportunities of the State to individuals who have acquired college level knowledge in ways other than through classroom attendance."[31]

Such testing services are vital to the structure of correspondence instruction. The correspondence student often finds that colleges or employers refuse to accept credit earned through correspondence programs. Since many such programs are derelict in offering proctored final examinations to validate student achievement, it is particularly difficult for the admissions officer or personnel executive to evaluate correspondence credits earned outside the formal system. These independent testing services ensure validation of achievement indicated by the student's performance under carefully controlled and supervised testing conditions.

FRAUD

The correspondence instruction market is wide open to fraudulent operators. Anyone or any group can become a correspondence instruction supplier. If the supplier is not concerned with the quality of his product, the cost of operation can be kept extremely low. He need not apply for voluntary accreditation, and he can frequently evade the regulatory authorities by changing the "school's" name and base of operations.

There are two basic types of fraudulent institutions. One type promises job opportunities which it cannot deliver. The Better Business Bureau of Metropolitan Boston has stipulated: "No school can 'guarantee' jobs to those taking its courses."[32] Invariably the student who enrolls in one of these courses has been the victim of what the U. S. Circuit Court of Appeals describes as "the customary hard sell." The other type is the diploma or degree mill which the U. S. Office of Education describes as "an organization that awards degrees without requiring its students to meet educational standards for such degrees established and traditionally followed by reputable educational institutions."[33]

The U. S. Office of Education feels that fraudulent instructional operations not only cheat the individual but create a bad image for American education abroad:

> Degree mills [are] a serious threat to American educational standards in several ways. They damage, by misunderstanding in the public mind, legitimate and reputable correspondence schools. They defraud those who honestly believe they have received recognition from a legitimate institution of higher education. They lower American prestige abroad by deceiving foreign students.[34]

To bring to light these unscrupulous operations, Dr. Ella Woodyard enrolled in a degree mill. With a total of only about 232 hours of work, she acquired bachelor's and doctor's degrees in psychology and a doctor's degree in philosophy. Dr. Woodyard comments:

> I wonder just what argument there can be, from the point of view of student advantage or public welfare, in favor of a school in which it is possible in less than a six-month period to obtain degrees that require at least eight years of hard toil in a resident university on the part of a superior student.[35]

The dimensions of the problem are more readily understood when one realizes that there are probably between eight hundred and one thousand private home study schools now operating in the United States of which only ninety-one were accredited by the NHSC at the end of 1966. Not many schools even seek accreditation. Of schools applying to the NHSC, about 50 percent are approved on their first application; another 25 percent receive eventual accreditation after correcting indicated weaknesses.[36]

Diploma mills offering some kind of watered-down instruction are an old phenomenon in this country, dating back more than one hundred years.[37] Despite regulatory efforts, they still thrive today. In 1960 the U. S. Office of Education issued "a preliminary list of more than 30 organizations designated as degree mills."[38] Robert H. Reid estimates that in 1959 more than two hundred such operations existed although not all were necessarily correspondence programs.[39] And in 1966 the Post Office Department reported that "the number of fraudulent correspondence schools operating in the United States has increased nearly 300 percent in the last three years."[40]

These fraudulent schools do grave damage to the legitimate correspondence schools. The poor name they give to correspondence instruction affects not only the private home study schools but the university programs and even the in-house training suppliers. The public is quick to associate correspondence instruction in general with the disreputable operators. If the legitimate suppliers want to avoid being associated with fraudulent schools, they must do all they can to see that the frauds are put out of business.

REGULATION

Control of education is not one of the powers expressly delegated to the federal government by the Constitution and accordingly is reserved to the states. However, the federal government can regulate correspondence instruction whenever fraudulent use of the mail or interstate commerce are involved.

Otherwise, regulatory activities are left to the states or to supplier organizations.

Our country's laissez faire approach to commerce contends that no business activity shall be regulated unless a clear social need for such regulation can be proved. The burden of proof always lies with the regulating body, thus providing a safeguard for free enterprise.

Suppliers of correspondence instruction whose offerings are ancillary to their main activities generally need no regulation. Instruction is supplied to those within the organization. The motive of promoting improved performance dictates an honest instruction program in the best interest of all concerned. Philanthropic suppliers do not need regulating either. They supply correspondence instruction free or at a minimal charge as a charitable activity. No one argues with such good intentions. Correspondence departments of universities are considered to be effectively controlled by the special climate and mores of the academic world, which provides its own traditions and rules. The Commission on Accreditation of Service Experiences provides the safeguards to ensure the quality of USAFI programs.

The need for regulation lies primarily within the broad range of private home study schools. When profit is the main objective, the risk of fraudulent operation is high. The NHSC attempts to regulate these schools through voluntary action, but it can only speak for its own members. Therefore federal and state governments have felt a need to keep careful watch over the private or proprietary suppliers of correspondence instruction.

The courts perform an important regulatory function each time they void a contract between a student and a fraudulent supplier or each time they convict a supplier of fraudulent practices. The law provides a guarantee to the student whenever he enters into a contractual arrangement. However, this type of regulation is greatly insufficient in several ways. First, it requires a certain amount of time, money, and legal sophistication on the part of the student if he is to successfully prosecute his case. Also, although the individual student may gain redress of his grievances, a court order canceling an individual contract provides no relief for all the other students bilked by the same fraudulent operation. Finally, by changing the school's name or moving it to a new location, as noted earlier, the fraudulent supplier can frequently begin all over again and make a healthy profit before being reapprehended. Thus, although the courts supply an indirect kind of guarantee to the student, they do not constitute an effective regulatory system.

The federal government through its agencies takes an active part in trying to halt fraudulent correspondence suppliers. One method of regulation is to specify which correspondence programs qualify as acceptable for students subsidized under the various GI bills. Congress has instructed the Federal Trade Commission (FTC) in the War Orphans' Educational Assistance Act of 1963 and the Veterans' Readjustment Benefits Act of 1966 to "aid the states to avoid approval for veterans' or war orphans' education or training of any school which uses advertising that is erroneous or misleading, either by actual statement, omission, or intimation."[41] Some federal loan programs also stipulate that the student must be enrolled in an accredited institution.

Correspondence schools operated as businesses are subject to all general laws pertaining to business engaged in interstate commerce as well as to provisions of the postal laws prohibiting the use of the mail to defraud. The Federal Trade Commission is the most significant regulatory body from the point of view of correspondence schools, the vast majority of which are involved in interstate commerce. The commission has published *Trade Practice Rules for the Private Home Study Schools,* describing unfair methods of competition and illegal practices. Violation of these rules may lead to initiation of appropriate proceedings by the FTC and result in a cease and desist order to stop such unfair practices. From 1952 through the early part of 1966, the FTC had issued seventy-five such orders to correspondence and vocational schools.[42] However, the FTC does not have the resources to prosecute successfully all the instances of false advertising or malpractice. Nor can it act when a school operates entirely within the borders of a single state. The commission flatly states that its

> authority to stop the use of unfair or deceptive practice by correspondence . . . schools which sell courses of instruction in interstate or foreign commerce is not adequate to assure adherence to minimum standards of quality from an educational standpoint.[43]

The Post Office Department (POD) has a particularly strong weapon to use against fraudulent operations: it can deny them use of the mail, thus crippling their operation. But before it can do so, the offending schools must be formally charged with using the mail to defraud. Thus the POD, like the courts, can only regulate after the crime has been committed. When the crime has been proved in court, the offender may be given a jail sentence and the Postmaster General may deny his organization use of the mail. But the Post Office Department is primarily concerned with distributing the mail, not with acting as a policing agency. It can only provide limited regulation through postal laws.

The state governments have the most potent regulatory powers. A state can grant or withhold corporate charters and revoke the charters of fraudulent operations. Under its authority to protect its citizens a state may also regulate any business to which it grants a charter. Actually, about half the fifty states have initiated some form of regulation over correspondence schools. Many states attack the problem of regulating private home study schools through licensing. The state stipulates conditions under which a school must operate to obtain and keep a license and requires all correspondence suppliers to have such a license.

However, a state may run into difficulty if it attempts to enforce similar licensing conditions on schools chartered in other states. The courts may hold such practice to be an undue burden on interstate commerce according to a precedent established by the U. S. Supreme Court in a 1909 ruling against the state of Kansas. A similar problem may arise when a state tries to require salesmen employed by schools chartered in neighboring states to meet its own state licensing requirements. Although a state may require a license for salesmen employed within the state, the "mere solicitation of orders by salesmen when acceptance and finalization of the offer occurred beyond the state does not constitute such business activity as to subject the firm to the state's jurisdiction," according to a court decision.[44] Unfortunately, some states have enacted no legislation at all to curb the fraudulent correspondence school. These states provide havens for degree mills which achieve nationwide distribution from these bases.[45]

CONCLUSION

The problem of regulating correspondence instruction completes the full circle. CERP explained in the introduction to what extent all the supplier problems are closely related. Financial needs determine the ability to obtain qualified staff for correspondence programs. Financial goals frequently play an important role in determining the attitude a program will take toward student enrollment and guidance. The problem of gaining acceptance for correspondence instruction both affects and is affected by the ability of a program to hire administrators, course writers, and graders, and to attract students.

In Chapter 4 CERP analyzes the potentialities of the correspondence method in order to establish what its inherent strong and weak points are as a method of instruction.

NOTES

1. Stuart Edward Beyer, "Cost Analysis of a Continuing Governmental Project with the Naval Correspondence Course Program as an Example," unpublished master's dissertation, Graduate School, Union College, Schenectedy, N.Y., 1965, pp. 72–76.

2. *NHSC News*, vol. 4, no. 7 (Washington, D. C., July–August, 1965), p. 3. Estimates were made by Warren B. Smith, President of LaSalle Extension University, in a report on a survey of 100 large companies.

3. *Report Submitted by the Legislative Research Council Relative to Private Correspondence Schools*, The Commonwealth of Massachusetts, Boston, Mar. 5, 1962, p. 70.

4. Renée Petersen and William Petersen, *University Adult Education: A Guide to Policy* (New York: Harper & Brothers, 1960), p. 92, quoting Cyril O. Houle, Introduction, *Universities in Adult Education*, p. 13.

5. Chester Allen and Charles A. Wedemeyer, *Extending to the*

People (Madison: University of Wisconsin Extension Division, 1957), p. 20.

6. Thorstein Veblen, *The Higher Learning in America: A Memorandum on the Conduct of Universities by Business Men* (New York: B. W. Huebsch, 1918), pp. 191–192.

7. Abraham Flexner, *Universities: American, English, German* (New York: Oxford University Press, 1930), pp. 144, 147.

8. Letter to CERP from G. O. Allen, President, Cleveland Institute of Electronics, Nov. 8, 1966.

9. Lyman Bryson, *Adult Education* (New York: American Book Company, 1936), p. 119.

10. National Home Study Council, *Business Standards*, Section V, Oct. 8, 1962, p. 4. (Mimeographed.) "Each accredited school must have a definite and established policy for the settlement of cases where students request discontinuance of training, but which shall not require such students to have paid, or to pay, amounts in excess of the following:

a. For students requesting cancellation and/or refund before their enrollment applications have been received and officially accepted and recorded at the home office—no charge; all monies paid by the applicant to the school or its representatives shall be refunded.

b. For a student requesting cancellation and/or refund within 90 days from the date of his enrollment—an amount not to exceed $50.00 plus 25% of the list price of his course.

c. For the student who requests cancellation and/or refund after 90 days from the date of his enrollment, but prior to the expiration of 180 days from that date—an amount not to exceed $50.00 plus 50% of the list price of his course."

11. Commonwealth of Massachusetts, *op. cit.*, pp. 42–43.

12. John S. Noffsinger, *Correspondence Schools, Lyceums, Chautauquas* (New York: The Macmillan Company, 1926), p. 16.

13. Commonwealth of Massachusetts, *op. cit.*, p. 30.

14. *Million Dollar Directory, 1966* (New York: Dun & Bradstreet, 1965). Private home study schools listed as having over $1 million net worth: American School (p. 52); Famous Artists Schools (p. 418); National Radio Institute (p. 897); National Technical Schools (p. 900); International Textbook Company, of which International Correspondence Schools is a division (p. 659).

15. Harry L. Miller, *Teaching and Learning in Adult Education* (New York: The Macmillan Company, 1964), p. 224, quoting a personal communication from Paul Sheats, Dean of the University of California Extension.

16. See Table 4–5, p. 177.

17. Petersen and Petersen, *op. cit.*, p. 139.

18. "Profile on Home Study," *Overview*, vol. 3, no. 8 (August, 1962), p. 32.

19. B. LaMar Johnson, "Footnotes on the Junior College: Guidelines and Trends in Post-Secondary Vocational-Technical Education," *Phi Delta Kappan*, vol. 46, no. 8 (April, 1965), p. 379.

20. Gayle B. Childs, "Can We Really Teach Well by Correspondence?" Research Concerning Supervised Correspondence Study, *The Bulletin of the National Association of Secondary-School Principals*, vol. 36, no. 190 (December, 1952), p. 12.

21. Thelma Gruenbaum, "The Personal Equation in Correspondence Teaching," *Adult Leadership*, vol. 7, no. 9 (March, 1959), p. 268.

22. Wayland J. Chase, "Teaching by Mail," *Proceedings of the NUEA*, vol. 2 (April, 1916), p. 64.

23. Grant Venn, *Man, Education, and Work* (Washington, D.C.: American Council on Education, 1964), p. 144.

24. *Review of Legal Education* (Chicago: American Bar Association, Fall, 1964), p. 21.

25. "Correspondence or Directed Home Study," U. S. Office of Education (OE-13002-64), March, 1964, p. 1.

26. William K. Selden, *Accreditation, A Struggle Over Standards in Higher Education* (New York: Harper & Brothers, 1960), p. 6.

27. *Statement of Criteria for Recognized Accrediting Agencies* (Washington, D.C.: National Commission on Accrediting, n.d.), p. 2.

28. Noffsinger, *op. cit.*, pp. 89–90.

29. *Opportunities for Educational and Vocational Advancement* (Washington, D. C.: Commission on Accreditation of Service Experiences, American Council on Education, 1965), Bulletin No. 10, p. 31.

30. *Ibid.*, p. 4.

31. *Credit by Examination* (Albany: The State University of New York, 1963), p. 3.

32. *Facts You Should Know about Home Study Schools* (Boston: Better Business Bureau of Metropolitan Boston, Inc., 1959), p. 15.

33. "Degree Mills," U. S. Office of Education, Division of Higher Education (Release OE-54015), March, 1961.

34. *Ibid.*

35. Ella Woodyard, *Culture at a Price* (New York: American Association for Adult Education, 1940), p. 101.

36. CERP telephone interview with William A. Fowler, Assistant Director, National Home Study Council, Nov. 21, 1966.

37. Commonwealth of Massachusetts, *op. cit.*, p. 75.

38. "Degree Mills," *op. cit.*

39. Robert H. Reid, *American Degree Mills* (Washington, D.C.: American Council on Education, 1959), p. 7.

40. *The New York Times,* Nov. 27, 1966, p. 60.

41. Letter to William D. Carey, Executive Assistant Director, Bureau of the Budget, from Paul Rand Dixon, Chairman, Federal Trade Commission, Washington, D.C., Apr. 14, 1966, *Proposal by the Federal Trade Commission for Enactment of Uniform State Laws to Regulate Correspondence and Vocational Schools,* FTC Proposal No. 3, p. 1.

42. *Ibid.,* p. 4.

43. *Ibid.,* p. 2.

44. Commonwealth of Massachusetts, *op. cit.,* p. 60.

45. *Ibid.,* p. 81. "The absence of sound educational standards in Illinois (prior to 1961), Indiana and Missouri make these States the headquarters for activities of the underworld of American higher education. Over two thirds of the active degree mills listed in a recent U. S. Office of Education bulletin operate out of these three states."

4

An Analysis of the Correspondence
Method of Instruction

THIS chapter begins with an examination of the instructional technique that actually defines corespondence instruction. Then, in turn, CERP examines the good points and the shortcomings of the correspondence method and concludes with an appraisal of selected correspondence courses. This chapter should be of interest to critics and supporters of correspondence instruction alike and should also answer many of the questions from readers who are unfamiliar with the method.

THE INSTRUCTIONAL TECHNIQUE

Recall CERP's definition of instruction, given in Chapter 1: "(1) a conscious, deliberate effort (2) to affect or alter the environment of an individual in such a way (3) as to cause him to behave or be able to perform in some given manner (4) and to do so under specified conditions." This definition corresponds to certain activities that make up the correspondence process.

CERP recognizes five stages of development in the instructional process: (1) planning a course, (2) preparing and presenting the course, (3) providing student-instructor interaction, (4) reinforcing and validating learning, and (5) revising the curriculum.

Planning a Course:

In planning a correspondence course there are five steps which can be briefly outlined as follows:

1. Analyzing the objectives and determining how they can be best accomplished by correspondence instruction

2. Specifying the objectives of the course in terms of desired terminal behavior

3. Specifying what characteristics are expected of students who will take the course and devising a method of determining whether a particular student qualifies

4. Specifying course content, based on objectives and student characteristics

5. Establishing criteria for successful completion of the course

ANALYZING THE SUBJECT What is there about this subject that can be best taught by correspondence? What aspects will be particularly difficult to teach by correspondence, and how can the planner best overcome these difficulties? A correspondence planner may decide that only part of the course can be taught adequately by correspondence: a course in surgery or advanced chemistry by correspondence might wisely emphasize theory and leave the student to gain practical experience through other instructional methods. No hard and fast rule stipulates that all courses should be all-inclusive; it is always advisable when possible to limit a course to what can be best taught through a particular approach.

SPECIFYING OBJECTIVES Deciding exactly what the course should accomplish (in terms of interim or terminal student behavior) is one of the planner's most important tasks. Before he can instruct his staff clearly about their particular responsibilities, the planner must establish a set of specific course objectives. Robert F. Mager, in his book on preparing instructional objectives, states: "I cannot emphasize too strongly the point that an instructor will function in a fog of his own making until he knows just what he wants his students to be able to do at the end of the instruction."[1]

Establishing course objectives—for any kind of instruction —necessitates defining the intent of the course. What will the student do when he understands the instructions and sets out to follow them? "Understanding elementary algebra" is not a satisfactory course objective. It is too vague and fails to indicate a specific action that is sought. "Solving quadratic equations" would be a much clearer objective.

Course objectives are extremely useful guides for the student. He is more likely to perform well when he understands his task clearly than if he has only an imperfect concept of what behavior is expected of him. Mager goes so far as to suggest: "If you give each learner a copy of your objectives, you may not have to do much else."[2]

SPECIFYING THE STUDENT The course planner should determine for whom the course is intended and then develop procedures to ensure that the right people take the course. Seemingly, this should not be an inherently difficult task. However, the correspondence course planner has a set of considerations quite different from that of the resident school administrator for specifying his student population: there are many situations in which the specifications cannot be administered satisfactorily by mail except at great expense.

The characteristics of the entering student for whom the course is intended may involve a range of conditions, knowledge, abilities, and skills. In one respect, they represent the qualities with which a student is already equipped. In another respect, they involve the student's readiness or willingness to do what the instructional plan demands of him.

In preparing instructional materials, the course writer, who is sometimes the course planner, must have in mind course objectives and the characteristics of the student population to be instructed. From these he can determine course prerequisites, the pace of the course, and the profundity of the instruction. The same approach cannot be used successfully to teach American history to college seniors and to eighth-grade students.

The problem of specifying the student is closely linked to the problem of enrollment. Correspondence programs that specify what students they wish to instruct must still determine how to tell whether the individual satisfies those qualifications and how to screen out those who should not take the course.

The practice of academic institutions in stating course prerequisites is, in a sense, one way of specifying the student. Actually, prerequisites may bear little relationship to the material to be taught in the course for which they are designated. A far more satisfactory approach would be to indicate quite specifically the pertinent characteristics and conditions of the population from which the student will be admitted.

Correspondence schools with wide-open admissions policies can be thought of as using a marketing approach in specifying the student. The prospective student is assumed to know what he needs to learn and to be able to judge whether the course will meet his requirements. Many times prospective students simply are not in a position to evaluate a course or to know what skills, abilities, attitudes, and knowledge are required to take it. Often they are sold a course rather than measured for it by specific, established criteria.

SPECIFYING COURSE CONTENT   The course content is the actual altered environment that stimulates the change in a student's behavior. The term includes both material (books, visual and aural aids, practice equipment, etc.) and nonmaterial content (the range of subject matter). Although he is not responsible for establishing the desired environment, the course planner must see that the subject matter corresponds to course objectives and student capabilities and that the means for altering the environment are satisfactory and feasible within the financial and technical limits of the program.

ESTABLISHING CRITERIA FOR SUCCESSFUL COMPLETION   What terminal behavior will be expected of the student at the end of the course? The planner can answer this question only after he has determined course objectives, specified student characteristics, and considered the content of the proposed course. Usually there will be a range of acceptable behavior between 60 percent and 100 percent (traditional school figures) comprehension and ability to perform in the desired way. Whether a person satisfies these criteria is usually determined by a combination of teacher appraisal, lessons submitted, and examinations. In correspondence instruction, the instructor is rarely able to give an adequate estimate of the student's achievement based on direct observation. Therefore, added weight falls on lessons and examinations. Those correspondence programs which fail to give adequate terminal examinations risk falling short of producing the desired student behavior. The planner should at least establish criteria for the desired terminal behavior so as to clarify the objectives of the course and permit eventual examination to determine whether that behavior has been learned.

Preparing and Presenting the Course

Once the course has been planned, the course writer must set to work producing it. He must be skilled in the subject matter to be taught and sensitive to the particular problems of correspondence instruction. Correspondence instruction relies much more heavily on the written word than does classroom or lecture instruction. Thus the course writer has an even more important task than does the ordinary textbook writer.

Frequently the correspondence course writer and course instructor are not the same person. The course writer must predict student problems and try to solve them within the structure of the course. There are several booklets available on how to write a correspondence course. Several of the better suppliers have developed their own.

The course writer must also face certain practical limitations. His product will usually be distributed by mail so he must often stay within certain volume restrictions. He must be aware of the capabilities of the grading system used by the particular supplier. It is foolish to demand elaborate responses from the student if they will not be carefully examined. In short, the course writer's task requires him to transmit course objectives and establish a learning environment for students he will never see and do so within the limitations imposed by the particular supplier for whom he is working.

THE CORRESPONDENCE TEXT Few commercially prepared texts are suitable for use alone as correspondence texts; however, many can be used in conjunction with carefully prepared correspondence materials. Suppliers either use standard texts or develop their own textual material.

SYLLABUS AND STUDY GUIDE Typically, specially prepared study materials are included in the course. They may accompany or replace the text. In one program they may be called syllabi and in another study guides, but their function is basically the same: to provide content and form for the instructional process. The general purpose behind the correspondence syllabus or study guide is to get the most out of the written word through special organizational techniques and attention to the special task of teaching at a distance.

The syllabus or study guide may combine the content of a textbook with the structure of lesson plans or serve as nothing more than an annotated guide to the text. Typically, provision is made for student participation in the instructional process through self-tests, lessons to be submitted, and problems to be solved. Wedemeyer and Childs describe the syllabus as follows:

> The syllabus sets forth the objectives of the course and of its subdivisions, provides for over-all organization, directs the students to sources of information, indicates reading to be done and activities to be carried out so that the purposes may be achieved, provides information supplementary to that to be secured from other sources, explains difficult concepts, intro-

duces new ideas, and indicates reports and other evidences of achievement which are to be submitted to the correspondence study department.[3]

As these two authors are particularly concerned with university correspondence instruction, they emphasize the use of other sources of information. However, in many correspondence courses, the syllabus itself contains the bulk of the textual content.

SUPPLEMENTARY MATERIALS Supplementary materials can be anything from supplemental readings to complex laboratory kits. Although the course writer rarely has to prepare the supplementary materials himself, he is often responsible for suggesting or requesting them. He may feel, for example, that verbal behavior cannot satisfy all the course objectives. He may then write part of the syllabus to include visual or laboratory aids.

Working supplementary materials into a program presents particular practical difficulties for the correspondence administrator. He must find ways of packaging, shipping, and perhaps processing these materials without putting undue strain on his program's resources. However, the creative possibilities of these materials present a tremendous opportunity for the course writer to improve his course. In fact, successful introduction of some of the innovations in instructional media (to be discussed at length in Chapter 5) may help correspondence instruction overcome many of its shortcomings.

SEQUENCING MATERIALS Organizing textual and supplementary materials into a coherent course is perhaps the course writer's most difficult task. He must determine the proper sequence not only of the information to be conveyed but of the process by which he expects the student to learn it. Thus sequencing demands both extensive knowledge of the subject matter and a grasp of the psychological principles of education.

New methods of sequencing have stirred up considerable controversy in recent years. In particular, the concept of programmed instruction with its detailed sequence of step-by-step advancement has had an important influence on teaching patterns. Although programmed learning has not been totally accepted by educators, it has certainly stimulated wider recognition of the importance of course sequencing.

MOTIVATING STUDENTS Students can be motivated to achieve course goals, but this is only one kind of motivation. The course writer can also help motivate the student by the way in which he structures the course. The stimulation of different senses and the variety offered by the use of audio-visual aids or other supplementary materials generally augments student interest.

Psychologists have also attempted to show that proper sequencing has a high motivational value. Logical development of a course often motivates a student by helping him to understand more easily, thus encouraging him to advance. This encouragement is especially important for the correspondence student who is studying independently. He runs a greater risk than other students of being slowed down or stopped by incongruities or particularly difficult steps.

PRACTICE AND REINFORCEMENT Educational psychologists point out that simply learning the material is not enough. An instructional program must also attempt to ensure retention of what is learned through practice, reinforcement, and testing. Otherwise the student's learning, produced by hard work from the supplier and the student alike, may dissipate shortly after each lesson.

Thus a course writer should be expected to include opportunities to practice and repeat skills or information learned in earlier lessons. Proper responses by the student must be encouraged and reinforced while faults are pointed out and the faulty behavior extinguished. The rigor of examinations often helps foster greater retention by forcing the student to review and preventing him from treating each lesson as a separate fragment that can be forgotten as soon as it has been completed.

PRESENTATION AND FORMAT   Some correspondence program directors argue that course presentation and the physical format of the syllabus are among the most important motivational stimuli to students. It is extremely important that the physical presentation of materials be carefully considered. For example, mimeographed materials and poorly done illustrations may seriously reduce the impact of well-presented ideas.

Providing Student–Teacher Interaction

The instructor or teacher performs the task that distinguishes correspondence instruction from the various forms of home study. He must provide the personal guidance and instruction that the student would expect to receive in a resident institution, but he must do so from afar. He must try to quiet the critics of correspondence who feel as Karl Jaspers does that "the printed lecture, perhaps even taken down word for word, is only a pale residue."[4] In general, correspondence suppliers consider the instructor's task to be the single most important constituent of the correspondence method. Ripley Sims, author of a U. S. Armed Forces Institute booklet, writes: "No study guide, regardless of how well written, can ever completely replace the educative give-and-take between the able teacher and his student in the really effective teaching-learning process."[5]

The USAFI instructor's manual "Guidelines for the Course

Instructor" gives one definition of the task of the correspondence instructor:

> Instruction by correspondence is thus seen to be much more than "fee grading" of lessons or reports by the correspondence instructor. The instructional process involves discerning properly the sincerity of the student's earnestness, assessing student progress toward objectives sought, recognizing and discovering the student's learning difficulties and providing the necessary guidance for overcoming these difficulties. Stimulating and challenging the student to further learning effort, and comprehensively evaluating the quality of the student's learning and assigning a lesson grade to estimate learning progress are also necessary in correspondence instruction.[6]

CERP recognizes four parts to the instructor's task and describes them as (1) preparation, (2) evaluation, (3) feedback, and (4) personal attention.

PREPARING FOR INSTRUCTION As noted above, the course writer and the instructor are frequently different persons. The instructor's first task, whether or not he has written the course, is to familiarize himself with the syllabus or study guide. He must be sure he can answer all the questions in the various lessons and tests. But he must go further and be able to predict and answer potential questions which the students may pose. The correspondence instructor does not have to worry about saving face before a class, but he must at least know where to find the answers to questions students may ask.

EVALUATING STUDENT WORK The instructor receives the student's lessons. He must have the knowledge and the ability to make complex judgments about the student and about the course from these responses. He may be asked to grade the student's work, but frequently he must go beyond simply recognizing errors. He must evaluate the student's work with the intention of improving the student's future performance. He must assess the student's likelihood of achieving course objectives and try to determine in what ways his performance may be deficient.

At the same time, the instructor must try to evaluate in what ways the course is a successful instructional device. Only after he has determined how well the course is succeeding in advancing the student toward course objectives can the instructor decide exactly how to help the student in difficulty. At the same time, he can determine how to improve the course and make suggestions that may lead to effective changes.

PROVIDING FEEDBACK The only contact the student has with the instructor is through feedback from the lessons he submits. CERP considers feedback a critical part of the instructional process. Without feedback there can be no real instruction (which is not to claim that there can be no *learning*. A student can learn from nature, experience, or a book without having been instructed.)

The teacher structures his evaluation of the student lessons and sends a copy to the student. These comments are frequently written right on the corrected lesson sheets. The instructor indicates errors and corrects them. The principle behind feedback says that a student cannot learn effectively by simply reading and then answering some questions. He must receive an evaluation of his work in order to reinforce his successful behavior and avoid repeating mistakes.

GUIDING THE LEARNER The personal attention the instructor gives to each student's problems is really a part of feedback. It consists of an instructor's evaluation being handed back to the student in the form of suggestions of various kinds.

The instructor may decide that the student does not show

sufficient motivation, perhaps through neglect, to submit lessons regularly. The instructor could write a personal letter to the student in order to encourage him to improve his performance. He might also write encouraging comments on the lessons he returns. On the other hand, he might try to motivate a sloppy student into doing more careful work by making severe comments and criticizing his carelessness.

The instructor must teach students with widely varying educational backgrounds, different intellectual capabilities, and different instructional goals. The supplier runs the risk of instructing them all poorly if he fails to give personal guidance to each learner. Thus the instructor carries the brunt of the responsibility for making the course fit the student, perhaps the most difficult task within the correspondence method.

Reinforcing and Validating Learning

Tests and examinations serve important functions in correspondence instruction. They force the student to reconsider the material he has studied. Subsequently he must be able to formulate written responses to precise questions. The student's responses allow the supplier to grant or withhold approval of his work in the form of certification or credit. At the same time, examinations indicate to the supplier the effectiveness of the instructional program.

REINFORCING THE STUDENT   The student who simply reads a book frequently forgets much of what he has read at the beginning by the time he reaches the end. The challenge of examination postpones and hopefully overcomes some of this decay. The student reviews and perhaps does extra work to prepare himself. He must be sure of his knowledge and have it available for instant reference during the examination. The stringent demands of examinations thus serve to reinforce learning.

VALIDATING ACHIEVEMENT The grader may have to evaluate written responses to subjective questions, criticize paintings or photographs or other nonverbal materials submitted as part of the course, or simply be able to read a grading grid. A grader affixes a grade to the student's work but is not expected to make suggestions to the student.

The grader performs the task that indicates whether the student has satisfied course objectives. If he has, the grader will advise the supplier to award him credit for the course. If there are subjective questions to grade, the grader must be skilled and knowledgeable. Typically, however, validation in correspondence programs consists of nothing more than mechanical grading of objective questions to determine a simple percentage of right and wrong answers. Thus validation is often a simple check-off procedure.

CHECKING COURSE EFFECTIVENESS Without some kind of final examination, it is very difficult for the supplier to know whether his course objectives have been achieved. Most courses involve cumulative changes in the student's behavior, and although interim changes are important, the student's final performance generally determines whether he has succeeded or failed.

For the supplier who seeks to train members of his own organization, such a terminal examination would seem necessary, unless some other measure of performance is used, to control the quality of the instructional program. For all suppliers who offer courses to the public, such terminal examinations still seem highly desirable. They help the supplier to decide what changes must be made to improve course offerings and what techniques seem to be the most successful.

CERP commends all those suppliers who offer proctored terminal examinations and strongly recommends their introduction by all who do not. Proctored examinations offer the best means of validating a student's achievement and detecting cheating or other student malpractices. Such examinations are in the best interest of supplier and student alike and should be given careful consideration by every supplier despite the considerable demands they make on the supplier's budget.

Revising the Curriculum

The course evaluation based upon the results of both lessons and interim and terminal examinations as well as the dropout rate should indicate how existing courses must be changed to make them more effective. Administrators, writers, and instructors who keep up with new developments in their academic specialties should be able to bring and keep courses up to date. But how does a supplier determine when to offer a new course, and what determines which courses he will offer?

EXTERNAL REQUESTS   Sometimes a business firm, school, professional association, or government agency may ask a supplier to create an outside course for them. Frequently student demands, as expressed in letters, surveys, or remarks to salesmen, stimulate a supplier to offer a new course. Those suppliers who determine a student's ability to take a course by his desire to do so are the most eager to respond to such requests, but all suppliers must be somewhat sensitive to the needs of their student body.

MARKET APPROACH   Some suppliers determine what courses
to offer by making a careful analysis of what the market will
bear. They look at how many courses in the same subject are
being offered, and they look at the demand for the particular
kind of instruction. Sometimes suppliers are accused of creating
the course first and making a market for it afterward. Certain
promotional techniques have been successful in selling courses
even when there was no previous demand. Schools seeking to
make a profit from their offerings are the most likely to create
new courses in this way.

NEW NEEDS   From time to time the structure of man's
knowledge changes in such a way as to demand the introduction
of new courses or reorganization of old ones to meet demands
for the new knowledge. Scientific developments are especially
likely to create new demands on instructional suppliers, but
no subject is immune to this kind of radical change. Changes
in armaments, equipment, and military techniques have an impact on training needs in the Armed Forces.

FULL CURRICULUM   Many correspondence suppliers check
their competitors' catalogs to determine what courses are being
offered. They may use this information to fill out their own
curricula or merely to meet specific competition. This practice
tends to foster course duplication rather than helping to meet
actual instructional problems with new approaches.

BENEFITS OF THE METHOD

Proponents of correspondence instruction claim that it can
perform certain instructional activities better than traditional
methods. Furthermore, they argue, it can instruct in some ways,
places, and situations in which no other method can instruct

at all. CERP analyzes the correspondence method in order to determine just what these advantages are and how they benefit the student, the supplier, and the entire educational system. In this section CERP examines claims that correspondence instruction is more (1) flexible, (2) economical, (3) psychologically sound, and (4) instructionally effective than other methods.

Flexibility

Resident instruction typically requires the student to conform to certain institutional demands. He must be at a specified place at a specified time in order to participate in the instructional process. The intellectual level and rate of advancement of the course are either arbitrarily fixed or determined by the teacher's assessment of the combined abilities of all the students in a particular class. In some ways, correspondence instruction is much more flexible than resident instruction, permitting the student to find his own level and satisfy his own instructional needs at his own pace. Moreover, he can choose when and where to study. This flexibility may convince the student of the advisability of taking correspondence instruction when he could not otherwise participate in an instructional program.

LOCALE Access to correspondence instruction is as available as the nearest post office or mailbox. Students tied to a particular locale where no resident instruction is offered may find correspondence courses the ideal response to their needs. Some states, such as Alaska and North Dakota, use correspondence programs to reach students who live too far from resident centers to be brought by bus to school each day. The Insurance Institute of Canada believes, "There is no better method of teaching people engaged in the insurance business in a country the size and with the spread of Canada."[7]

People who move frequently from place to place also find it difficult to meet the demands of resident instruction. The Armed Forces use correspondence instruction to train a shifting military population; businesses often use it to provide in-service training for salesmen or traveling representatives. Students who hesitate to enroll in resident courses because vacations, job responsibilities, or a permanent change of address may interrupt their studies can enroll confidently in a correspondence program and take their school with them.

PACE   All students do not learn at the same rate. Some are able to move ahead rapidly; others need time to reread lessons and understand difficult points. Yet resident classes are governed by the necessity for all students to advance at approximately the same rate. Educational psychologists are becoming increasingly concerned with the consequences of molding the student to fit the system instead of creating a system that can meet the demands of the student. They point to the waste resulting from holding a fast learner back because the class cannot keep up with him or from foolishly trying to push a slow learner beyond his capabilities.

Even the individual does not learn all subjects or all lessons at an equal pace. He should be free to devote as much time to each lesson as he needs to understand it. Correspondence instruction allows the student to work at his own pace. Although he may receive encouragement from the supplier, the student ultimately determines his own working speed. The fast learner, for whom the opinion makers recommend increased use of correspondence instruction, can finish a course in a short time; the slow learner can devote the extra care to study that he needs.

One should not confuse the problem of allowing each individual to proceed at his own pace with the problem of coping with differences in the capacity of individuals to learn. Given a lifetime, some students would not be able to complete some courses simply because the courses may not be adapted to their individual capabilities.

COURSE CONTENT Experts continue to debate whether all subjects can be taught by the correspondence method. Noffsinger claimed that a school must be judged not only by "its maintenance of standards but by the nature of its curriculum. If it offers certain courses, it misleads the student, however honest its intentions."[8] Yet supporters vaunt the "practically unlimited variety of subject matter"[9] which can be taught through correspondence at every intellectual level. In fact, they claim, there is no discipline in which correspondence instruction cannot be used; some subjects can be better taught by correspondence.[10] The correspondence method is readily adjustable to any educational situation.[11]

CERP does not give unqualified support to these claims of the adaptability of the correspondence method to any subject matter. Although perhaps any subject could be taught by correspondence, all cannot necessarily be taught well by the method. Neil F. Garvey takes an impartial look at the problem of adaptability of course content in a paper on university correspondence instruction:

> There is, perhaps, no more crucial problem facing the correspondence administrator and the academic departments involved than that of determining which of the course offerings of the institution may be appropriately taught by correspondence. Academic subjects vary widely with respect to their suitability for instruction by mail. No responsible official connected with home study would claim that all subjects lend

themselves equally to the home study method, nor that all subjects can even be taught in this manner. In many instances the requirements of elaborate and expensive laboratory facilities, the necessity for guidance in the development of specific intricate manual skills, or the extensive employment of pure discussion techniques within a group may dictate the necessity of some other mode of instruction. On the other hand, many subjects lend themselves most admirably to the home study method.[12]

CERP recognizes that a large variety of subject matter can be taught by the correspondence method and considers this flexibility an advantage. At the same time, suppliers are warned to examine the demands of each subject closely before choosing to offer a course by correspondence instruction. Adaptability of content remains an advantage only so long as it is not misused.

USE AS A SUPPLEMENT Correspondence instruction need not be used alone. In fact, the correspondence method is easily adapted for use with other instructional methods (see Table 4-1, page 153). Thus it can be used to supplement other instructional methods, or other methods can be used to supplement correspondence instruction. In very large classes, correspondence instruction may be used to improve student-teacher contact. One young lady, enrolled in a lecture course at a large Midwestern university, took the very same course simultaneously by correspondence because "this was the only way she could get any feedback from her professor on the papers she wrote."[13]

Correspondence courses have been used with notable success in business for pretraining. Before beginning a training program or going to a conference, the student takes a preparatory correspondence course. The course may review prerequisite information for the training program or prepare the student for discussions at the conference. This technique can be readily adapted to other preparatory instructional tasks.

Correspondence instruction can also provide supplementary instruction to the person otherwise occupied. A young executive-in-training may be told he needs some legal, accounting, or management background beyond what his training program offers. He can pick it up through correspondence instruction without interrupting his training or can acquire it after he begins work.

Economy

Some argue that it costs less to provide correspondence instruction than to provide resident instruction. For example, they say that the cost of building and maintaining resident facilities may alone be greater than the cost of an entire correspondence program serving an equivalent enrollment. But economy is a relative matter. CERP hastens to point out that correspondence instruction can only be compared to resident instruction if one accepts the premise that they supply roughly equivalent quality instruction. No matter how inexpensive, nothing is a bargain unless the quality of the merchandise is acceptable. And when well done, correspondence instruction can be more expensive than equivalent residence instruction.

INITIAL COST   CERP has already indicated how the low cost of initiating a correspondence operation can tempt fraudulent operators to open sham schools. On the other hand, the low cost of establishing a program also serves to encourage the use of correspondence instruction. Both the supplier and the student may be attracted by the low cost of correspondence instruction: the supplier to set up a program; the student to take courses. When the cost of resident instruction is beyond the means of the student, correspondence instruction may provide a useful alternative.

OPERATING EXPENSES   Because of the low initial cost of setting up a correspondence program, a proportionally higher part of a supplier's funds can be directed toward running the instructional program. CERP surveys have shown that instructional costs (largely staff salaries) make up the largest expenditure in the budgets of most types of suppliers. Only in competitive private home study schools in which advertising and promotional costs cut heavily into the budget do instructional costs fall to second place.

Operating costs (excluding advertising) for correspondence instruction generally run well below those for resident institutions. However, costs mount as suppliers pay increasing attention to the individual student and his problems. If the student (or the taxpayer) were to pay a fee for correspondence instruction comparable to what he pays for resident instruction, the supplier could offer many more personal services. Instead, most correspondence programs continue to function as poor man's schools, largely serving those who cannot afford more expensive instructional programs.

SUPPLY AND DEMAND   Giving a resident course necessitates supplying a teacher and a classroom. The same need exists year after year although one year thirty students may take the course and the next year only five. As correspondence courses need no classrooms and as instructors and graders are typically paid by the lesson, there is never any waste of space or manpower.

Furthermore, there is no need to assemble all the students at one time. Whereas scheduling difficulties, work shifts, or teaching loads might necessitate several sections of the same course in a resident institution, a single correspondence course can accommodate them all. Students moving at different rates of advancement can take the same course simultaneously without causing scheduling problems.

TIME   Correspondence instruction is particularly economical with the student's time. He may work whenever he wants. Frequently students fit their study time in around other activities. Some students may study while putting in time at some other occupation. Recuperating patients frequently find correspondence instruction an ideal way to put their period of convalescence to good use; housewives with young children may try to continue their studies while raising a family.

CONTINUING TRAINING   An estimated 75 percent of all vocational training through correspondence ties in directly with the student's job. Employers must constantly train and retrain employees to keep them abreast of developments in management or technology. But a steel mill or insurance company cannot stop operation every six months to send its employees to school. Instead it can provide correspondence programs that the employees can complete without leaving the job. The dual goals of continued production and continued training are compatible when the training is conducted by correspondence.

In the U.S.S.R., where the government is particularly concerned with increasing production, correspondence instruction plays an important role.[14] Students and workers perform the necessary task of producing the goods demanded by the Soviet society. These same students and workers continue to study through correspondence combined with on-the-job training or resident schooling without interrupting production. They satisfy their own instructional needs and help the economy develop at the same time.

EASING PRESSURE Correspondence instruction can prove economical to a resident system. Sometimes by integrating a few correspondence courses into a resident program, a school system can avoid hiring new teachers to meet marginal demands. Supervised correspondence programs in small or isolated school systems frequently help overcome temporary problems or bridge the gap until permanent solutions can be arranged.

Psychological Soundness

The correspondence method has certain psychological advantages over other instructional methods. These qualities attract many students to correspondence programs. CERP notes that correspondence instruction seems especially well suited to the psychological needs of the former dropout and to the radically different needs of the aggressive seeker after knowledge.

REGAINING CONFIDENCE The dropout or flunk-out from resident instruction often finds he cannot reenter a resident institution. Either the school refuses to take him back or the student is unable to overcome the feeling of failure he associates with resident instruction. For such a student, correspondence instruction may provide an acceptable way to acquire the desired academic standing and regain confidence.

There is no class with which to compete and no classroom to evoke memories of past failures. The correspondence student can choose his study environment and work quietly in his own way. He can prove himself by performing well. As many correspondence programs use complimentary grading techniques, he may be encouraged by high grades. In any case, the lack of pressure in the correspondence method is likely to prove beneficial to the student who has lost confidence through previous failure.

FEAR AND EMBARRASSMENT   Many students have a great fear of embarrassment or failure, which keeps them from performing well in resident classes. For fear of making an error, a student may never participate in class discussions and thus never get adequate feedback on his performance. Adult learners may actually refuse to enroll in programs of continuing education out of fear of embarrassment before their neighbors. Some children may build up a fear of being criticized or embarrassed in front of their peers which will mark them in all their further learning activities.

Correspondence instruction largely avoids this fear of failure. No one but the student need know how well or how poorly he does. The student is encouraged to study for his own benefit, not to impress others.

NATURAL SELECTION   Correspondence suppliers also bring up the rather dubious argument that the correspondence method performs a kind of natural selection, weeding out those who should not be students and leaving only highly motivated and capable learners. They point out that the aggressive seeker is clearly the student best-suited for correspondence study and the one most likely to succeed.

However, this opinion contradicts their claim that most dropouts are not failures, and it takes an oversimplified view of the problem of nonstarts. Although CERP recognizes that highly motivated students are likely to perform better than others, it does not accept the claim that correspondence instruction necessarily separates the outstanding students from educational riffraff. A more judicious claim is that students who do well on correspondence programs display a certain tenacity and ability to follow through that stand as good recommendations of the student's disposition to work.

Instructional Effectiveness

As pointed out earlier, all these advantages are of little use if correspondence instruction does not provide effective instruction. But as educators still disagree on how to go about measuring instructional efficacy, CERP must rely largely on testimonials and the opinions of experts for its judgment.

BEST AVAILABLE METHOD   Many users of correspondence instruction who are reluctant to give an unqualified judgment of the effectiveness of the method nevertheless defend it as the best available method in many particular situations. Implicit in this defense is the consideration that the best available method must be at least satisfactory in itself to justify its use.

Flexibility, economy, and psychological advantages, as indicated above, often make correspondence instruction the best available method. For the isolated, extremely poor, or easily embarrassed student, correspondence instruction may be or appear to be the only available method. In many other cases, users compare relative merits and choose correspondence instruction for its particular benefits. On the other hand, "several companies specify that correspondence school courses may be approved only if appropriate instruction is not available to an employee on a classroom basis,"[15] and a CERP survey shows that only 3.6 percent of responding large businesses and industries use correspondence instruction in preference to other instructional methods, while 24.4 percent use it only as a substitute method (see Table 4–1).

Kenneth B. Hoyt sums up the "best available" position with a rather low appraisal of the correspondence method:

Very few people, including those who sponsor them, would claim that home courses as an approach to education for employment are equal to or better than classroom study. They are, however, defended as a means to self-improvement for those for whom other avenues are not available.[16]

Rossi and Johnstone, in their CERP report, note that as the only method available, correspondence instruction "would come to be viewed as an appropriate and perhaps even attractive alternative."

TABLE 4-1

Use of the correspondence method by 250 large companies

OUR COMPANY USES CORRESPONDENCE INSTRUCTION:	PERCENT OF RESPONDING COMPANIES*	RESPONSES
In preference to other methods	3.6	9
Only as a substitute method	24.4	61
In combination with other methods	75.2	188

* This column adds to over 100 percent because some of the 250 companies indicating use of correspondence instruction responded in more than one category (e.g., used only as a substitute, in combination with other methods). Some of the 250 made no response to these categories.

SOURCE: CERP survey of the 500 largest United States industrial corporations and the fifty largest banks, life insurance, merchandising, transportation, and utility companies as listed in *Fortune Directory*, August, 1964. (Survey conducted in 1965.)

SATISFIED USERS   Opposing these lukewarm appraisals of correspondence instruction are the hundreds of allegedly unsolicited testimonial letters from satisfied students. Many students listed as dropouts write in to explain that the instruction was so successful it allowed them to achieve their desired goal before the end of the course. Some private home study school directors who frequently use testimonial letters in their advertising claim that some letters are so complimentary as to be useless for publication: "No one would believe we did not make them up ourselves." Students praise the care instructors give to each lesson submitted, the clarity of course objectives and sequencing patterns, and the advantages of being able to work at their own pace. "Study by correspondence allows me to progress at my own pace, as my time permits," wrote a young man whose work in the controller's office of his company required him to travel extensively. CERP checked the student's record and found he was progressing well in his course. He had indeed proceeded at his own pace. His record showed bursts of activity with several lessons submitted at once interspersed among extended periods of inactivity.

Many organizations that use the correspondence method also express their satisfaction with it. The CERP survey of large businesses and industrial corporations indicates that over 64 percent of those responding find correspondence instruction an

TABLE 4-2

250 large companies evaluate the correspondence method

OUR COMPANY CONSIDERS CORRE-SPONDENCE INSTRUCTION TO BE:	PERCENT OF RESPONDING COMPANIES	RESPONSES
An effective instructional method	64.8	162
An ineffective instructional method	8.4	21
About the same as other methods	24.4	61

SOURCE: CERP survey of the 500 largest United States industrial corporations and the fifty largest banks, life insurance, merchandising, transportation, and utility companies as listed in *Fortune Directory*, August, 1964. (Survey conducted in 1965.)

"effective method," while less than 9 percent consider it "ineffective" (see Table 4–2). Many organizations use it to fill certain needs or in conjunction with other instructional methods. The Armed Forces demonstrate their acceptance of the method by their widespread use of correspondence instruction to meet their training needs.

EMPIRICAL STUDIES Several empirical studies have attempted to compare the performance of correspondence students to that of students who have studied primarily in the classroom. A typical approach to such comparisons is to match test scores on independently administered examinations. Examiners frequently attempt to control such variables as sex, IQ, and age, but little work has been done in examining the significance of such variables as motivation and whether the student has chosen his own method of instruction. The usual difficulties in determining the validity of the tests administered and defining the results also contribute to casting considerable doubt on the empirical results that examiners would have us accept as proof. Gayle B. Childs gave this résumé of empirical results in a paper delivered in 1965:

> At the high school level, a study by Meierhenry showed no difference in performance on standardized tests by students studying vocational courses by correspondence study and those studying the same courses in regular classrooms. Studies by Hanna and Childs indicate that students who study by correspondence perform somewhat better on standardized tests than do students of equal ability who receive instruction in the classroom. Another study by Childs shows that students who take mathematics courses by correspondence study in high school receive higher grades in their initial mathematics courses in college than do students of comparable ability who study mathematics in high school by classroom methods. A

study by Sjogren shows no difference in achievement between students who study by correspondence study and those who study the same content by programmed instruction. A series of studies at the University of Nebraska over a period of 3 years and involving a variety of subjects showed no difference in achievement between students who studied by a combination of correspondence study and television and those who were enrolled in the same subjects in regular classrooms.

At the college level, studies by Zeigel at George Peabody College, Schwin at the University of Colorado, and Larson at the University of Arizona found that correspondence study students make higher grades than do classroom students. The study by Zeigel equated the groups on the basis of ability.

Studies by Crump at Teachers College, Columbia University, Kingsbury at the University of Chicago, and Sorenson at the University of Minnesota, compared the test scores of correspondence study students with the test scores of students of comparable ability who studied the same subjects in regular classrooms and found no differences in achievement.

It is interesting, and I think significant to note the consistency of these findings. All show that correspondence study students learn at least as well as do classroom students. There is no evidence to the contrary.[17]

Inasmuch as the studies of the effect of correspondence instruction have generally not been rigorous, great care must be used in interpreting the results. At least, however, they do demonstrate that students can learn something about some subjects by the correspondence method as measured by standardized achievement tests. They do not show, in spite of this, that every subject or that all aspects of a particular subject can be taught well by correspondence or that the result of teaching a subject by correspondence is necessarily better than or inferior to teaching it by another method. Finally, these studies do not adequately compare the effectiveness of teaching by correspondence with teaching by other methods, and they fail to disprove the possibility that correspondence students who complete their courses are so highly motivated that they will learn in almost any instructional situation.

A much more reasonable conclusion to draw is that under some circumstances correspondence instruction can provide the environment needed to allow a student to meet certain instructional requirements. Correspondence instruction will prove most useful when the supplier (1) is aware of the method's capabilities, (2) determines the requirements for teaching the particular subject which must be met in order to achieve course objectives, and (3) compares correspondence instruction with alternative methods and ascertains that it is the most appropriate method for presenting the course under consideration.

Other Instructional Advantages

Supporters of correspondence instruction add a few instructional advantages of the method to those listed separately under "Flexibility." The four listed below, part of a list compiled by Clem O. Thompson,[18] stress the rigor of independent study and the necessity for putting questions and answers into writing. Thompson claims such practice forces the student to clarify his own thinking and do a more thorough job when studying by correspondence.

1. The student must express himself at every point in the course; more thorough preparation is needed throughout the course.

2. The student does his own research and checks his own

work; this requires initiative and persistence and results in self-discipline and self-reliance.

3. The student has a greater opportunity to present the subject matter fully and to write understandingly, which requires clear thinking.

4. Students in doubt are more willing and ready to ask questions as they go along.

Advantages in Training Personnel

Table 4–3, displaying the results of a CERP survey, reviews the advantages of the correspondence method cited by officials of large United States companies.

TABLE 4-3

250 large companies rate advantages of the correspondence method

CORRESPONDENCE INSTRUCTION HAS THE ADVANTAGE OF BEING:	PERCENT OF RESPONDING COMPANIES	RESPONSES
Inexpensive	26.8	67
Flexible	56.4	141
Convenient	71.2	178
Preferred by employees	9.2	23
Available to any size group	50.0	125
Useful in other ways	35.6	89

SOURCE: CERP survey of the 500 largest United States industrial corporations and the fifty largest banks, life insurance, merchandising, transportation, and utility companies as listed in *Fortune Directory*, August, 1964. (Survey conducted in 1965.)

General Usefulness

Many educators, particularly those directly involved in correspondence instruction, feel that the correspondence method needs no apologies. F. T. Wilhelms, a leader in the movement at the University of Nebraska, told a receptive audience at the First International Conference on Correspondence Education:

> The keynote of this conference has been emphasis on the fact that correspondence education is not a stop-gap or a temporary expedient, but a genuinely sound method of education. The members of the conference have accepted the responsibility of providing, by correspondence, an opportunity for education which is complete, well-rounded, and wholesome.[19]

Leaders in correspondence instruction do not hesitate to claim that "the real potential of the correspondence course method is yet to be felt."[20] They see correspondence instruction as "not merely an off-shoot" but "an equal which, if properly used, will carry its own weight in meeting a significant part of the educational requirements of the nation."[21] One specialist predicted a bright future for correspondence instruction "because the educational demands of this century cannot be met without it."[22] Arthur Klein, former executive secretary of the NUEA, is frequently quoted from an article he wrote in 1920 for a U. S. Bureau of Education *Bulletin*. Klein gives one of the strongest statements of the general usefulness of the correspondence method for quality instruction:

> Practically all of the courses given in college and high schools and many that are not can be and are taught by correspon-

dence. *Much of this work can be done to better advantage by correspondence than in residence.* For example, in research work the resident student must make investigations and reports. For this class of work the ending of the classroom hour and the fact that the work must be completed by a fixed date makes correspondence study far more reasonable and practicable. It is impossible to parcel out such work into 50-minute periods or terms of fixed length, *and for highest grades of educational work correspondence study methods are universally used.*[23] [Italics added.]

CERP recognizes certain limitations on the usefulness of correspondence instruction; some critics go further and criticize its usefulness in any situation. CERP judges correspondence instruction to be generally useful when the techniques for creating and operating a correspondence program, as outlined in the first part of this chapter, are diligently applied and when the limitations to be discussed in the following pages do not impinge too seriously on the suppliers or the students involved in the correspondence program.

SHORTCOMINGS OF THE METHOD

Although correspondence instruction profits from some particular advantages over other methods, it also has its share of special problems. CERP described problems external to the method in Chapter 3; in this section of Chapter 4, CERP fulfills its promise to examine problems inherent in correspondence instruction.

Some of the problems have already been mentioned briefly: specifying students, guiding and motivating students, and validating student achievement. Many others are examined here for the first time, such as lack of physical facilities, limitations of the written word, and lack of interaction among students.

CERP recognizes five different categories of shortcomings in the correspondence method: (1) problems of working at a distance, (2) special limitations, (3) dependence on the written word, (4) physical handicaps, and (5) lack of acceptance of the method. They account, in part, for the poor reputation correspondence instruction has among academics and for some of its instructional failures. CERP examines these shortcomings in order to determine corrective measures and suggest improvements.

Working at a Distance

The distance that separates the correspondence student from his instructor provokes serious instructional problems. Despite efforts by many conscientious suppliers to overcome these difficulties, the problem of student "loneliness" remains one of the principal drawbacks of the method. Correspondence instruction lacks the interchange of student views and ideas that stimulates and accelerates student development. Working at a distance also makes the task of incorporating student reaction into courses particularly difficult. Most important of all, the correspondence method forfeits the warm personal contact between student and teacher and imposes a geographical and temporal distance between them.

STUDENT–INSTRUCTOR INTERACTION CERP recognizes student-instructor interaction as the heart of the correspondence method. This interaction is absolutely vital to instruction; when it falters, the quality of instruction necessarily declines. Yet inherent in the remoteness of student and instructor are certain problems that make this interaction extremely difficult to achieve.

During the early years of correspondence instruction, critics warned that student loneliness could negate any advantages of the method: "Systematic study generally requires the stimulus and corrective of living touch with the teacher."[24] CERP has shown that close attention to lessons submitted and conscientious feedback of corrections and suggestions can help overcome the lack of "living touch." Charles A. Wedemeyer emphasized the value of this form of interaction in an article in *The Home Study Review*:

> Correspondence courses that make use only of check-off type lessons or examinations at the end of each assignment—with only a grade report to the student—actually deprive the student of instruction. Such devices no doubt are more economical, but the chief value of the correspondence method lies in the tutorial relationship developed between the teacher and the student, and to minimize or destroy this relationship actually changes the character of the work offered. Thus, schools that depend solely upon the use of objective or machine-type scoring have abandoned what is generally regarded as "correspondence study." Such programs are in fact programs of "self study."[25]

But correspondence instruction cannot offer feedback as rapidly or as effectively as resident instruction. The student must always wait for his paper to be received, examined, and returned before he gets any feedback. Although two-thirds of the respondents in a CERP survey of 800 correspondence suppliers report that they provide feedback in seven days or fewer from the time they receive the student's lesson, this effort cannot begin to match the immediate response of a teacher in the classroom. Often feedback is most valuable at the point of error, correcting the student immediately and preventing him from learning wrong information or behavior. After seven days the student may experience considerable difficulty in changing a week-old pattern of thought or performance.

Similarly, student questions should be answered at the point of difficulty. A time lag of a week or more frustrates the student. The method may stifle student curiosity or curtail his interest by its inability to respond promptly to queries.

COUNSELING AND GUIDANCE

Home study cannot offer the well-rounded counseling possible on a regular campus. The student may face troubles quite outside his school assignments, and a counselor just a few minutes away could help him.[26]

CERP has already touched on the problem of providing adequate counseling by correspondence. Some programs make a concerted effort to provide guidance for their students. The Division of Supervised Study of North Dakota State University offers a free counseling service to all its students. Supervised correspondence instruction conducted within the boundaries of a single state can perhaps afford to carry out such intentions; a national supplier of correspondence courses to all who wish to enroll can hardly make the same offer. Yet the student may falter and eventually drop out of a course because he does not receive sufficient help. Students who study alone typically need more, not less, guidance than students who have frequent contact with their instructors.

WITNESSING PERFORMANCE Both students and instructors learn from watching each other. Students pick up attitudes from an .instructor's manner of delivery as well as from his actual class notes. Demonstrations and experiments in the classroom provide a model for the students to follow and are important instructional devices. It is impossible to relay the full impact of such demonstrations simply by describing them in writing or illustrating them with diagrams.

Teachers learn from observing student behavior. They can better evaluate a student's capabilities if they have the opportunity to watch him perform. They can also better judge the effectiveness of their own instructional techniques if they can witness immediate student reactions. Student behavior in laboratory experiments, public speaking, or playing the violin could all be photographed or recorded, but the process is generally too expensive to be practicable. As technological advances bring down the cost of audio-visual aids to instruction, their use in correspondence study will increase.

LACK OF INTERACTION AMONG STUDENTS Students learn from contact with each other. Informal student discussions and classroom debates have always been an important adjunct to the more formal student-instructor relationship. The desire to excel in the presence of their peers stimulates many students to greater achievements (although CERP recognizes that this drive is not an unqualified asset). Students can help each other individually or derive mutual benefit from group study. The correspondence student misses out on all these benefits.

Furthermore, many educators point out that young students learn to live in a social environment through contact with others their own age at school or college. Although this is not a direct criticism of the correspondence method, it may nevertheless be important to the young student who learns primarily by correspondence. Correspondence instruction is an instructional method, not a total educational experience. This limitation should be recognized by anyone advocating study exclusively by correspondence, particularly for young students.

INFLEXIBILITY IN REVISING COURSES   Working at a distance makes it difficult for the supplier to make changes in materials or in the instructional approach. Whatever approach the written course takes, the course content must be communicated effectively. A teacher can always readjust at the last minute if he sees that his students do not understand, but a printed text cannot respond to student difficulties. Although correspondence instruction has the advantage of permitting a student to proceed at his own pace, as noted earlier, it is inflexible in adjusting to differences in ability. Once a course has been printed it is difficult for the supplier to adjust the content to suit the individual capabilities of the students. This inflexibility of approach decreases the instructional merit of the method.

The mail-order system generally necessitates keeping a large inventory of printed materials on hand. New developments in the subject cannot be reviewed by the teacher in class, for there is no teacher; they must be printed and inserted in the old syllabus. If the changes are important enough, they may force an entire rewriting of the old syllabus. Discarding old materials and creating new ones of sufficient quality and quantity frequently cause the supplier considerable financial hardship. Hence, many suppliers do not revise often enough.

REGULATING QUALITY   Regulating the behavior of the student and the quality of his work from a distance is a difficult supplier task. CERP has already indicated some of the problems of trying to control enrollment without adequate personal contact with the applicants. Maintaining interest and preventing dropouts has also been discussed.

Maintaining standards customarily required in resident instruction is sometimes nearly impossible for correspondence suppliers. Because many suppliers do not offer proctored terminal examinations, they cannot be sure the student has been working honestly. Demanding uniform high standards from a student body that lacks the necessary background or intelligence is folly. Yet such a student body is the rule, not the exception, in correspondence instruction. As a result, the suppliers frequently find they must tailor their standards to fit their students. Such a policy naturally detracts from the quality of instruction a supplier can offer.

Special Limitations

Certain characteristics of the correspondence method impose limitations on its use. Not all subjects can be equally well taught at a distance, nor can all students learn equally well by correspondence. The supplier must take these special limitations into account before creating a new course.

SUBJECT MATTER A good rule of thumb to follow is: The greater the importance of physical performance in learning a subject, the less useful correspondence instruction will be in teaching it. Training a young student to be a surgeon involves instructing him in many new manual and technical skills. Even in a fully equipped hospital with all the necessary materials to work with, a young man could not satisfactorily learn all he needs to know about surgery through correspondence. A lawyer presumably could learn through correspondence all the case histories and all the legal terminology he must master, but no supplier could expect to teach a student argumentation or give him simulated courtroom experience by correspondence. Dean John G. Hervey of the Oklahoma City University School of Law adds that in correspondence courses in law "the emphasis is wrong. The basic purpose of a good law school is to teach law students—to teach them how to think and how to act like a lawyer."[27]

In courses in which extensive laboratory experimentation is necessary, the supplier must overcome the lack of necessary facilities before being able to offer the course successfully. In the U.S.S.R., mobile laboratories and resident laboratory facilities are made available at specified intervals to correspondence students. Even when the facilities are adequate for such courses, however, problems of observation, validation, and providing useful feedback are prodigious.

STUDENTS Some critics argue that not all students are capable of correspondence study. They point out that self-discipline and intelligence are prerequisites to self-help. Those who have difficulty following simple directions cannot expect to complete a correspondence course by themselves, nor can the student who lacks the motivation and assiduousness to sit down and work on his own initiative hope to satisfy the demands of correspondence study.

Labor unions have never been particularly active suppliers of correspondence instruction. Joseph Mire, who was executive director of the National Institute of Labor Education, gave the following explanation:

> Learning by correspondence courses is basically self-study and requires a measure of self-discipline and skills in learning which the ordinary worker did not possess. The change in educational level of workers over the past 50 years may well provide a better base today for self-study than existed previously.[28]

Mire also pointed out that correspondence instruction has

proved successful with workers in Great Britain, Germany, and especially Sweden.

Dependence on the Written Word

The written word is but one means of communication. It has its inherent restrictions and its particular advantages. Not all learners react equally well to written or printed materials. Printed materials are somewhat inflexible and frequently dull. Correspondence instruction relies heavily on the written word as a medium of instruction and as a means of communication between student and instructor; when a written text is limited or insufficient to the task, instruction can suffer to a serious extent.

THE STUDENT AND THE WRITTEN WORD   CERP has already pointed out that some students cannot rely exclusively on the written word for their training. Doctors, laboratory or field scientists, and lawyers were cited as examples. Those who must perform manual or oral jobs need to be trained in manual or oral behavior. As an extreme case, one could presumably teach the principles of rhetoric through a written syllabus, but it would be foolish to equate such teaching with complete training in public speaking. Gestures, inflections, and manner are extremely important parts of the public speaker's repertoire. They could be described but never adequately taught by the written word alone.

In addition, CERP recognizes the phenomenon of the aural or visual learner. Some students simply learn better by looking at examples or listening to explanations. They are handicapped when the written word is the only instructional medium used.

RIGIDITY The written syllabus organized into sequential steps does not leave much room for imaginative exploration. The student must follow along the pattern indicated by the text. The specific referential qualities of language impose certain limits on most written materials. The student is encouraged to understand what the texts mean rather than to explore the characteristics of various materials or situations. Trends in education are leading away from this rigidity toward more experimental programs.

TESTING Correspondence programs rely heavily on written lessons and examinations. As subjective responses are difficult and costly to correct, these programs frequently resort to objective testing. Such examinations are typically unimaginative and frustrate whatever desire the individual may have to express himself. They do not test his ability to express, to analyze, or to synthesize. Such testing devices are entirely unsuited for certain disciplines in which imaginative thinking is part of the behavior to be examined. Nor can written examinations of any kind fully validate the abilities of a mechanic, an actor, or a soldier. Proctored written examinations may be accepted as the best available testing method, but suppliers and the public should realize the limitations implied. Another serious problem facing suppliers is the cost of proctored examinations. They tend to avoid their use; thus student performance does not receive adequate evaluation.

Physical Handicaps

A resident institution supplies certain facilities. Traditionally schools and colleges are equipped with laboratories, libraries, gymnasiums, theaters, and rooms reserved for tranquil study.

Correspondence instruction must operate without such facilities, and this limits its potential effectiveness in certain subjects.

LABORATORIES   Rigorous science courses frequently require some kind of laboratory experience as part of the course work. A degree in science implies the ability to perform certain laboratory activities. Correspondence suppliers may either expect the student to find laboratory facilities (on the job or perhaps at a resident institution) or send him some rudimentary equipment. As even simple laboratory equipment is expensive, the latter practice is not very common. More frequently the student can expect to find his laboratory equipment replaced by the following instructions: "As you read this section, imagine yourself in a laboratory actually performing the experiment."

Language laboratories are somewhat more easily adapted to the correspondence method. The student need only have access to a tape recorder to be able to participate in an elementary language laboratory experience. As these machines become less expensive and more readily available, the feasibility of using them for language teaching by correspondence increases.

LIBRARIES   The Division of Supervised Study of North Dakota State University runs a lending library for its correspondence students. However, such practice is a rare exception. The cost and operational difficulties of such a program would discourage most well-intentioned suppliers. After all, they contend, the student usually has access to a public library in his own community. Nevertheless, the correspondence student is at a real disadvantage in not having at his disposition a well-stocked institutional library catering to his specific needs.

TRANQUILLITY   The resident student can make use of study halls and libraries when he needs a quiet place to study. If he is in college he probably has a quiet dormitory room of his own and access to study centers on campus. But the worker or businessman who studies by correspondence may have to study at home. Frequently the home is not the tranquil environment needed for optimum study. Disruptive noise and activity can put the correspondence student at a disadvantage and discourage him from finishing his program.

Note: Although correspondence instruction cannot provide gymnasiums, student cafeterias, or social centers, they can hardly be criticized for not doing so. Only those zealots who would claim that correspondence instruction can provide total education on a par with resident institutions will have to defend the lack of these facilities.

Lack of Acceptance of the Method

Correspondence instruction definitely must compete with other methods for the scarce instructional and financial resources it needs to survive. Critics argue that the correspondence method has too many drawbacks to deserve a share of these resources. They cite the advantages and availability of better instructional methods. To make correspondence instruction good enough to compete with resident methods, they claim, would make the cost prohibitive.

AVAILABILITY OF OTHER METHODS   Correspondence instruction still reaches many isolated students and brings instruction to many who would otherwise be deprived of an opportunity to study. But, in the United States at least, such cases are decreasing. As school systems become better organized and transportation becomes easier and more rapid, an increasing number of students are finding their way to the resident centers of learning. The spread of junior colleges and adult education centers has brought continuing education to many who previously might have turned to correspondence instruction. There will always be some for whom study through correspondence is the only possible method, but correspondence instruction cannot hope to grow and prosper on their numbers alone.

THE PRICE OF EXCELLENCE   CERP has shown how teaching at a distance poses many serious problems for the conscientious supplier. In many cases these problems are not insuperable, but to overcome them requires an enormous investment by the suppliers. First they must pay for research

TABLE 4-4

250 large companies rate disadvantages of the correspondence method

CORRESPONDENCE INSTRUCTION HAS THE DISADVANTAGE OF HAVING:	PERCENT OF RESPONDING COMPANIES	RESPONSES
Slow instructor feedback	41.6	104
Low employee completion rate	32.0	80
Employee questions go unanswered	20.8	52
Low employee motivation	19.2	48
Lack of stimulus of group study	73.4	186
Other problems	24.0	60

SOURCE: CERP survey of the 500 largest United States industrial corporations and the fifty largest banks, life insurance, merchandising, transportation, and utility companies as listed in *Fortune Directory*, August, 1964. (Survey conducted in 1965.)

on the problems; then they must pay to create the solutions; and finally they will continue to pay in most cases throughout their operation because these solutions require more expensive materials and greater shipping costs. It is possible that the cost of maintaining excellence in correspondence instruction would force many of the suppliers out of business. And those who ultimately will finance these changes, the students, must decide whether the increased cost can be met without tipping the balance in favor of other methods. The student and the taxpayer will watch carefully to see whether their dollars are bringing in enough value to justify continuing support.

GENERAL DISAPPROVAL   Little is known about which methods actually instruct well and which do not. Apparently educators are among the first to claim that the correspondence method is not really effective (see above, pp. 103–105). Even companies that use the method are often critical of it (see Table 4-4). Some of their complaints summarize criticisms made earlier in this chapter. Both students and teachers seem to feel that the lack of personal contact is a towering obstacle to effective instruction. Perhaps the most condemnatory cut of all is this quote from a Texas teacher who instructs both resident courses and correspondence courses:

> I do not consider any course that I give by correspondence as valuable as a course in residence. Certainly I should be able to add more to the course in residence, make more explanations, better corrections, and more applications.[29]

If people who work in both systems feel this way, then correspondence suppliers have a long way to go before they achieve their Messianic hope of complete acceptance of the method.

AN APPRAISAL

To investigate the kind of job correspondence suppliers were doing, CERP interviewed many schools and reached many more by questionnaire. Subject-matter experts were invited to evaluate a number of selected courses currently being offered through correspondence. The majority of the courses were chosen from offerings of private home study schools and universities rather than from supplier groups with special interests or restricted student bodies. The schools whose courses were sampled are considered to be among the better suppliers of correspondence instruction.

In evaluating the courses, reviewers were asked to consider the following points:

1. Clear definition of course objectives for student

2. Relationship of instructional materials to course objectives

3. Procedures to provide student with feedback or information on his learning

4. Organization of course materials

5. Clarity and adequacy of instructions to student

6. Physical format of materials

7. Appropriateness of technical content for level of learning stipulated for the course

8. Correctness of technical content

9. Consistency of material with current knowledge (up to · date)

10. Proctored general examination

11. Suggested improvements for the course

Comments by reviewers ranged all the way from those which found courses excellent on practically all counts to criticism suggesting a course was so poor it should be completely redone. There were, however, two important impressions presented by the reviewers. Many of the courses reviewed were not considered to have been very well done. Reviewers found many of them weak on points such as modernness of technical content, course organization, physical format, student requirements, student-instructor interaction, and final examinations.

The second general point brought out by the reviews was that the criticisms of weaknesses were not influenced by the fact that these were correspondence courses. If all the inadequacies mentioned were corrected, the courses could still be offered satisfactorily by correspondence. Examples of recommended improvements included the use of more up-to-date materials, better methods for reproducing the study guides, better organization of materials, more challenging assignments, more and better student-faculty interaction, and the enrichment of courses with more outside reading.

Clarity in Defining Course Objectives

Reviewers had been asked to comment on the extent to which the course made its objectives clear. In some of the courses they found course objectives well and clearly defined, but the dominant theme of their reports was one of dissatisfaction. Some indicated that the title was a little ambitious when compared with the objectives. Some found the objectives merely implied through the title or through the introduction. One comment, fairly typical of many, was:

The course objectives are clearly stated; however, no attempt is made to point out the limited scope of this course compared with radiation shielding technology. This oversight is compounded in that the title of the course . . . is not an accurate reflection of . . . [its] limited scope.

In a few cases reviewers found there was really no statement of objectives at all. A reviewer in biology said, "I cannot find anywhere a clear statement of the objectives of the course."

Generally there seems to be an indication that in most cases there is an effort to state, for the student, the objectives of the course. The major problem seems to be too great a reliance on title or subject and in some cases reliance on catalog statements which are usually far too brief. Another somewhat general problem is inconsistency between the title and the objectives.

Course Materials and Course Objectives

The reviewers tended to rate most courses favorably on the relationship of instructional materials to course objectives. Usually when the objectives were clear, the course material was relevant to those objectives. The one noticeable criticism was that in some cases, when the material was not considered consistent, the title and objectives were usually just too ambitious for the instructional materials offered.

Feedback to the Student

Nearly all reviewers noted a very serious effort to provide the student with some information as to how well he was doing in the course. This was as true of those courses which provided no proctored final examination as it was of the others.

Many of the courses required the student to do written work which was to be turned in, graded, and returned to him. The typical pattern consisted of solving problems, answering questions about the reading material, reporting on experiments or other projects, and sending in evidence of direct efforts to apply what had been learned in the course.

Among the suppliers responding to a CERP survey (see

TABLE 4-5

Answers to the question, Which of the following do you use in at least half of the subjects offered by your organization's program of correspondence instruction?

ITEM	NUMBER ANSWERING	PERCENT OF TOTAL (231) ANSWERING
Objective tests, examinations, or problems	174	77.4
Subjective tests, examinations, or problems	158	68.4
Devices to stimulate students who are not submitting their lessons within a reasonable period of time	165	71.4
Letters to the student discussing his work each time he sends in a lesson or examination	86	37.2
Comments on graded tests, examinations, or problems returned to student	208	90.0
Other (please specify)	35	15.5

SOURCE: CERP survey of 800 suppliers of correspondence instruction from which 231 responses were received. (Survey conducted Winter, 1964, and Spring, 1965.)

Table 4–5, page 177), a large proportion reported that they provided comments on graded papers, an indication of their serious awareness of the problem of keeping the student informed of his progress. In spite of the real effort to provide students with feedback, the reviewers felt that under the correspondence instructional method a student's progress too often is not satisfactorily evaluated. Materials required of the student were not generally of the sort to provide the teacher evaluating his work with a very satisfactory basis for informing him of his progress.

This view was supported by other data collected by the project. They showed a heavy reliance on objective tests, clerically or mechanically graded, which reduce costs and can increase speed in returning materials. When subjective methods are used, the grading is often either too lenient or perfunctory. The self-check schemes provided by some courses were considered by reviewers to be quite helpful in some cases; in others, reviewers found them too simple to be of real value.

It should be emphasized that the reviewers as a whole did indicate that they believed feedback and student evaluation could be done in the courses which they reviewed. They simply felt, for the most part, that what was being done was not being done very well.

Organization, Student Instructions, and Course Format

On the whole the reviewers were not too critical of the courses they reviewed when it came to the discussion of the organization of the materials. A few courses were thought to have been excellently done and a few very poorly done, but in most instances the reviewers felt that the materials were reasonably well organized. This would indicate that the people preparing the material had studied the learning task sufficiently well to arrange the materials into what most reviewers considered a logical sequence.

The courses also fared quite well on the procedures followed in instructing the student. The statement that the instructions were clear appeared over and over. There were the usual extremes, but on the whole most received a satisfactory reaction.

There was no marked agreement, however, that a generally good job had been done by most institutions on physical format. A minority, but still a sizable number of reviewers, felt that physical format had not been given enough attention. In some courses they found unappealing materials, not well-arranged physically and sometimes not too easy to read, which they felt would tend to inhibit a student's learning and perhaps discourage his future progress in his course.

Reviewers reported that some institutions provided a truly superior physical format in their course materials. A fine format, however, did not necessarily mean a course was rated high in other respects by the reviewers. The physical format of a psychology course study guide, for example, was described as "fresh and appealing. Type is very legible and spacing is very good. Occasional cartoons add to variety and interest." The textbook was considered "less commendable in these respects but still quite adequate." In direct contrast, the technical content of the course was judged "very badly out of date," the self-tests inadequate, and the course poorly organized. Overall, the course was rated as poor.

There were a few examples of the reverse situation as well in the courses reviewed, but for the most part reviewers found that a school which had prepared a course with fine technical content and instructional organization also took the trouble to see that it was not crippled by careless physical production.

Technical Content of Correspondence Courses

The reviewers treated the various aspects of technical content together. Generally, they considered correspondence courses quite weak in this category, not so much because the technical content was inaccurate as because it was sometimes not particularly appropriate or more typically it was simply not very rigorous or challenging and was too often out of date. Other than a few complimentary statements about those few courses considered excellent, the reviewers' comments left the impression that many of the courses were simply not as well prepared as they should have been. A very few of them said, in effect, "But what more can you expect in a correspondence course?" The majority, however, did not appear to have this bias. The points they criticized could be corrected within the traditional framework of correspondence instruction as many of their suggestions for improvement made clear.

A reviewer of several mathematics courses, after approving course objectives, format, and organization of materials, complained, "It is precisely because none of these courses adopts the attitude of the 'new math' that I find them all inadequate on the basis of contemporary standards." However, in respect to one course just released by a large private home study school, he added, "The course gives what would be considered by present-day standards a good modern background in the subject . . . and accords well with current practice in good schools."

On another course in another field, a reviewer commented,

The technical content of the course is appropriate for home study work; however, it is impossible to say whether it is an appropriate level of learning because of the vague set of goals presented. The technical content is reasonably accurate, but it should be more diverse. Both the textbooks were published in the 1950s. . . . There has been a tremendous explosion in the field . . . since the National Defense Education Acts; none of it is reflected in this course.

Two courses in real estate, one from a university and one from a private home study school, brought these comments from the reviewer,

In general, the instructional material was well organized to facilitate the learning process, and the technical content was presented accurately in a readily understandable manner, clearly and specifically related to the course objectives. . . . Several weaknesses [in both courses] with respect to the criteria concerning recent developments in the field were noted in the analysis. . . . Both institutions' courses were prepared within the last two years. Yet neither one contains information regarding innovations . . . or institutional changes, or the increasing awareness of local housing market research. or the application of modern management techniques in the real estate field.

The reviewer made "suggestions for the elimination of the weaknesses cited" after pointing out several sections in each which "appear to contain errors or are not clearly presented." In the covering letter accompanying his report, he commented:

My conclusion, based partially on this study, is that the present and potential usefulness of correspondence education is virtually unlimited. This potential has been enhanced by the development of rather inexpensive equipment, such as tape recorders and slide viewers, which may be effectively incorporated in the correspondence course.

The Final Examination

The course reviews as well as the institutional surveys indicated that although the majority of suppliers give proctored final examinations, there are still many who do not. Chief among the latter are the private home study schools. Several courses which were investigated and considered reasonably satisfactory in other respects failed to measure up, by criteria offered here, simply because they did not provide the proctored final examination.

Some courses, on the other hand, included final examinations which reviewers felt were not a satisfactory measure of whether a student had met course objectives. Two representative criticisms will be given as examples.

A reviewer of several college chemistry courses said of one of them which provided a purely objective examination:

> The examination is distinguished by its emphasis upon pure recall and by the remarkably small number of questions that demand anything beyond the merest ability to think, to demonstrate understanding. . . . The point is that good questions can be asked of the material . . . and that thoughtful, challenging questions, requiring more than simple recall, can be framed objectively. . . . It certainly does not meet the objectives set forth in the study guide. It overemphasizes a few of the topics covered in the text and omits many far more important topics completely.

A reviewer of a course in education said,

> The final examination could be taken by someone with a good liberal arts education who had done none of the reading

recommended or required. I cannot believe that the authors took a careful look at the examination in terms of the stated purpose of the course.

Summary

If we are to accept the comments of the majority of the reviewers, correspondence courses, with some shining exceptions, tend to have weaknesses. This can be attributed to four principal causes: a faulty concept of education, lack of knowledge of subject matter, lack of adequate resources, and relatively naïve conceptions of instruction as a technical process. On the basis of the courses reviewed, one can understand why correspondence education has a rather unflattering reputation. But it does not seem that this reputation is necessary. One certainly cannot conclude that instruction is not feasible through the correspondence method. One can conclude that there are serious problems which are not being met.

CONCLUSION

CERP opened Chapter 4 with an examination of the technique of the correspondence method. This examination is intended to provide a base for all further discussion of the method. CERP defined and described this process of instruction and roughly indicated the role of each of the members of the supplier's staff in preparing and operating the program.

But CERP feels that description by itself is insufficient. A useful survey must attempt to evaluate what it describes. CERP has tried to give an unbiased evaluation of the potential of the correspondence method. By examining the theoretical structure of the method, CERP has attempted to determine the inherent benefits and the inherent drawbacks of instruction by correspondence.

The results show that the method has both praiseworthy points and serious deficiencies. CERP believes that judicious use of the method can make the most of the advantages and minimize the faults. But the suppliers must be honest. They should not try to supply correspondence courses without first determining whether the particular subject can be appropriately taught by correspondence. Nearly any subject can be taught in part by correspondence; many subjects can be admirably taught by correspondence in their entirety. But CERP strongly encourages each supplier to look carefully at the nature of the subject, the qualities of the projected student body, the facilities available to his operation, and the capabilities of his staff before deciding whether to offer a course. Many suppliers would perform a greater service to education by withdrawing some of their poorer courses and concentrating on producing quality instruction in those they are best suited to supply.

In Chapter 5, CERP explores opportunities for correspondence instruction as a component of the instructional system and offers recommendations for increasing its effectiveness as an educational method.

NOTES

1. Robert F. Mager, *Preparing Instructional Objectives* (Palo Alto, Calif.: Fearon Publishers, Inc., 1962), p. 3.

2. *Ibid.*, p. 53.

3. Charles A. Wedemeyer and Gayle B. Childs, *New Perspectives in University Correspondence Study* (Chicago: Center for the Study of Liberal Education for Adults, 1961), p. 8.

4. Karl Jaspers, *The Idea of the University* (Boston: Beacon Press, 1959), p. 57.

5. Ripley S. Sims, "Preparation of USAFI Course Materials," U.S. Armed Forces Institute, Madison, Wis., June, 1960, pp. 4–5. (Mimeographed.)

6. "Guidelines for the Course Instructor," U.S. Armed Forces Institute, Madison, Wis., January, 1960, p. 18.

7. CERP interview with Thomas Roxburgh, General Manager, Insurance Institute of Canada, Sept. 4, 1964.

8. John S. Noffsinger, *Correspondence Schools, Lyceums, Chautauquas* (New York: The Macmillan Company, 1926), pp. 33–34.

9. Wedemeyer and Childs, *op. cit.*

10. CERP interview with Israel Sweet, Vice-president for Education, LaSalle Extension University, Aug. 26, 1964.

11. Gayle B. Childs, "Supervised Correspondence Instruction," in Charles A. Wedemeyer (ed.), *The Brandenburg Memorial Essays on Correspondence Instruction* (Madison: University of Wisconsin Extension Division, 1963), p. 28.

12. Neil F. Garvey, "The Status of University Correspondence Instruction: A Qualitative Approach," paper read at the Annual Southwest Conference on Adult Education, Austin, Tex., Oct. 11–13, 1959, p. 4.

13. Letter to CERP from Jones B. Shannon, Nov. 9, 1964.

14. Otto Peters, "USSR," *Der Fernunterricht Materialien zur Diskussion einer neuen Unterrichtsform*, vol. I, a publication of the Padagogisches Zentrum (Education Centre), Berlin Reihe C:

Berichte, (Weinheim und Berlin: Beltz Verlag, 1965). Also, "Correspondence Instruction," in I. A. Kairov and F. M. Petrov (eds.), *Educational Encyclopedia*, vol. II (Moscow: *Sovestkaya entsiklopediya* vol. I, 1964; Vol. II, 1965).

15. "What's New in Tuition-aid Plans?" *The Conference Board Record*, National Industrial Conference Board, Inc., vol. 1, no. 1 (January, 1964), p. 23.

16. Kenneth B. Hoyt, "Education as Preparation for Employment: Broadening the Base of Responsibility," *Educational Implications of Technological Change*, Report by the National Commission on Technology, Automation, and Economic Progress, Appendix IV, *Technology and the American Economy* (Washington, D.C.: U.S. Government Printing Office, 1966), p. 101.

17. G. B. Childs, "The Potential of University Home Study Programs," paper given at Brigham Young University, Provo, Utah, Jan. 14, 1965.

18. Clem O. Thompson, *University Extension in Adult Education* (Bloomington, Ind.: National University Extension Association, 1943), pp. 192–193.

19. A summary of group discussion by F. T. Wilhelms, *First International Conference on Correspondence Education*, Victoria, British Columbia, Aug. 22–24, 1938, pp. 185–186.

20. Robert Allen, "Farewell from the Editor," *The Home Study Review*, vol. 2, no. 3 (Fall, 1961), p. 5.

21. Russell V. Ritchey, "Correspondence Education in the United States Air Force," unpublished manuscript, Nov. 16, 1965.

22. Allen, *op. cit.*, p. 7.

23. Arthur J. Klein, *Correspondence Studies in Universities and Colleges*, Bulletin No. 10 (Washington, D.C.: U.S. Bureau of Education, 1920), p. 16.

24. H. J. Mackinder and M. E. Sadler, *University Extension,*

Past, Present, and Future (London: Cassell & Company, Ltd., 1891), p. 75.

25. Charles A. Wedemeyer, "Going to College at Home," *The Home Study Review*, vol. 4, no. 3 (Fall, 1963), p. 29.

26. L. V. Johnson, "Individual Professional Development through Home Study Programs," *The Home Study Review*, vol. 4, no. 4 (Winter, 1964), p. 61.

27. John G. Hervey, *Educational Requirements for Admission to Practice Law in California*, statement before the Interim Senate Judiciary Committee, Santa Monica, Calif., Sept. 29, 1964.

28. Joseph Mire, *Labor Education*, Inter-University Labor Education Committee, 1956, p. 155.

29. Lorenzo Zachery Timmons, "Correspondence Study for College Credit," master's dissertation, Texas Technological College, Lubbock, Texas, 1930, p. 73.

5

The Task for the Future

THIS chapter ties up the loose ends. The history and development of correspondence instruction are transformed into blueprints for future development. The benefits of the method are reexamined to determine how suppliers can use them to solve their instructional problems. Some new concepts are introduced to try to determine how to raise the present standard of instruction closer to the ideal. The following discussion also considers some innovations that could actually lead to expansion of the possibilities of the method beyond its present limitations. CERP concludes with some concrete suggestions on how the various suppliers can improve the quality of their instruction as well as their operational practices and their public image.

CERP subdivides this chapter into three main sections. The first examines some of the innovations in instruction that present an exciting challenge to correspondence instruction. The second section points out that to meet this challenge some of the supplier groups must begin to overcome traditional distrust and cooperate. The third section contains the specific CERP suggestions of changes which should receive priority attention.

THE CHALLENGE

The shape of instruction is changing. Even in the classroom the traditional student-teacher relationship is shifting under new pressures. Changing society has introduced new concepts in guidance and an entirely different kind of student into the schools and colleges. In the mid-twentieth century, science is responding vigorously to the challenge of creating new instructional media to meet the demands of an education-conscious society.

The New Media

CERP cannot hope to describe each of the intricate and interesting innovative media in detail in this study. The interested reader can consult the well-developed and rapidly growing library of books on the new media that is already available. However, CERP intends to mention and describe some of these media briefly in order to indicate their importance to the correspondence method. New media to be examined include (1) audio tape, (2) films and slides, (3) television, (4) video tape, (5) programmed instruction, (6) computer-assisted instruction, and (7) other media.

AUDIO TAPE Many subjects demand both oral and aural behavior (in addition to or in place of written behavior). Language study, drama, music, and public speaking are among the most obvious. To successfully complete a course in one of these disciplines, a student should be required to give some kind of specified performance which can only be evaluated aurally. The performance is necessary both for learning and for validation of the student's achievement. The tape recorder may be a useful instructional and testing tool in these situations.

CERP has also indicated the case of the student who learns particularly well from aurally presented material. He may read poorly or have difficulty visualizing when confronted with printed words. The tape recorder can help the student avoid these difficulties and also provide the tones and inflections missing from a written text. In addition, many students cannot read with any degree of comprehension as fast as they can understand a spoken (or recorded) lecture. A final advantage is that students often take notes much more easily and rapidly while listening to a lesson than while reading one.

FILMS AND SLIDES Films and slides satisfy the visual learner's need for a visual image. They can supply exact demonstrations in cases in which only proportional or representational models might be possible (e.g., a steel mill in operation). The camera can capture not only an event but some of the emotion of those participating as well. The new 8 mm film loops are easy to operate and inexpensive enough for extensive home use.

Films have the advantage of motion. They can reproduce an event or demonstration in uninterrupted form. Slides have the contrasting advantage of control. The viewer is not distracted by motion; he can concentrate on a single view while listening to a synchronized recorded lecture describing or commenting on the subject.

TELEVISION Some colleges and universities now cooperate with open-circuit television stations—both commercial and educational—to produce instructional programs. Frequently students are offered textbooks and sometimes a full course of instruction by correspondence to accompany the television sessions. Some universities have offered college credit to students participating at home in such programs.

However, an important potential for televised instruction lies in closed-circuit television. The instructional program does not have to compete with profit-making shows or general educational programming. The institution can direct specific instruction at a controlled audience through closed-circuit TV.

New developments in communication now permit the student to receive feedback from the closed-circuit television instructor. Telephone or two-way radio systems link the lecturer with all the classrooms. A student need only push a button, be recognized, and ask a question to receive instant feedback. Necessarily, the size of the class and the length of the lecture limit such possibilities; yet this interaction prevents the television from becoming a totally inhuman and unresponsive teaching device.

VIDEO TAPE Video tape offers two striking advantages over film: it needs no processing and it can be viewed on a fairly simple viewer. Because no processing is necessary, video tape is ready for replay as soon as it has been made. It can be used to review an experiment that would be costly or impractical to repeat. It can be used to illustrate a historical event while the event is still in the news. It is a flexible medium that can change a visual presentation much more quickly than a new film or slide series can be produced.

Video tape can be run through open- or closed-circuit television channels. If the reader is not aware of having seen television shows on video tape, he may at least be aware of the video tape replays of sports or news events. But video tape can also be viewed through special video tape viewers. Such viewers could be installed in libraries or study rooms and used by students in much the same way as many students are now accustomed to using microfilm. Then students would not be required to assemble at one time and one place to watch a tape as they now must do to view a film. They could arrange to view the material on video tapes at their own pace and convenience.

PROGRAMMED INSTRUCTION Programmed instruction is based on a principle of sequencing and reinforcing learning. A student progresses more rapidly and understands better when material is arranged in a consistent pattern. Small steps are easier to take than large steps, and so programmed instruction moves bit by bit into new material. The student gets practice at responding and using the new information by answering short questions at every step. Brevity and repetition are important concepts in programming.

The student fills in blanks in a printed program. These blanks correspond to a correct word or group of words. If the student responds correctly, the program will permit him to continue; otherwise, his mistake will be indicated immediately and subsequently corrected. Thus the student receives instant feedback on his learning. The program may come in the form of a book or a printed roll to fit into a special teaching machine.[1]

Although the above description is inadequate to explain everything about programmed instruction, it does cover the main points:

1. The programmed material is carefully sequenced.

2. Steps are kept simple and short.

3. Students respond (i.e., participate) in the process.

4. Responses receive some kind of immediate feedback.

5. Thus the student is corrected immediately and frequently given advice on how to correct his errors, or he is reinforced immediately for his correct answer and motivated to continue.

COMPUTER-ASSISTED INSTRUCTION The computer has exciting potential for use in instruction. Its ability to store information and feed it back at high speeds brings the computer closer to the potential effectiveness of the tutor or personal instructor than any other mechanical or electronic device.

Computers have already been used in conjunction with programmed instruction. The student typically sits at an electric typewriter console that is plugged into a central computer. The student types out a preestablished code to select the desired program, and the machine types out the first question. The student types in the response. If he is correct, the machine will perhaps congratulate him and then pose another question. If the student types an incorrect answer, the machine may correct him. Computers can operate on branching programs which may try to lead the student back to the correct response through a series of leading questions. This procedure helps the student understand in just what way his response was unacceptable and encourages him to analyze and correct his own mistakes.

Computers can also be used for learning games. Such games frequently consist of complex problems. Teams compete to supply the best solution with the computer deciding the winner. The College of Business Administration of The University of Texas organized one such game in which they created a fictitious company. Seven or eight business firms in each of several selected cities were asked to form teams from their managerial personnel. Each team received detailed information about the fictitious company concerning sales, costs, inventories, and production and limited information about competing teams. Each week the teams were to submit management decisions to cover a period of three months. The decisions were mailed to the university, where staff members fed the information into computers. Results were returned immediately to the teams, and the next week's decisions were based, in part, on the previous week's results. The game lasted sixteen weeks, squeezing nearly four years of "experience" into that short time.[2]

OTHER MEDIA The above-mentioned media do not begin to exhaust the techniques or means of communication in which educators are experimenting. The telephone has been used to link the student and his instructor. Stephens College in Columbia, Missouri, ran an unusual instructional program by telephone in which a number of colleges participated. Noted scholars in different parts of the country gave lectures in their homes or offices which were relayed to classrooms or lecture halls in the participating colleges. After the lecture, with a professor from Stephens serving as moderator, the students were allowed to question the lecturer—again by telephone.

The radio has frequently been used for instructional purposes. In Sweden, when English became part of the required school curriculum, radio courses supplemented correspondence study wherever qualified English teachers were unavailable.[3] The radio, combined with correspondence instruction, proved particularly useful in this case in which teachers were not readily available and the students needed to hear proper pronunciation in the unfamiliar language.

Many of these media are not new. Records, for example, have been used in the schools for many years. But the emphasis on audio-visual materials has grown enormously. As a result, many new ways to use the old materials have been developed, and new media have been created to overcome some of the limitations of the early audio-visual materials.

Aims of the New Media

The new media do not represent haphazard results of scientific advance. They have been developed to meet certain instructional needs. As the educational psychologist confirms a new learning theory, the scientist sets out to develop an instructional medium that will satisfy the demands of the new theory. Some of these innovations are meant to be part of an integrated resident system; other innovations are more flexible and can satisfy individual instructional needs without depending on a resident institution.

The pace at which a student learns is a major concern of educators. Audio and video tapes, programmed learning, and computer-assisted learning all cater to the individual student's speed and ability. As long as the necessary equipment is available, the student can arrange to use it when he is ready to learn. Previously the learning situation had been largely dictated by the practical necessities of assembling a class and an instructor in a classroom or lecture hall at a set time.

The new media can also provide higher motivation than traditional methods of instruction. Instead of appealing solely to the reading faculties of the individual, they stimulate several of his senses. Students are accustomed to think of watching films or television as pleasant activities. Although this attitude often presents some problems, it does help motivate the student to accept and participate in learning with the new media. Furthermore, programmed learning has motivational reinforcement built right into it. Programs are designed to motivate the student through a lesson by encouragement, sequencing techniques, and instant feedback.

In many ways the new media represent advances in economy over traditional instructional methods. They can reach an unlimited number of students. The supplier need only print more programs, make duplicate films or copies of the tapes, and add television receivers or computer consoles. The student can frequently work at home or in a nearby library. The new media are also economical with the time and energy of instructional experts. The best instructors or the experts in a subject need not repeat the same lecture many times to reach many students. The new media can record a lecture once and play it back an indefinite number of times all over the world. Instead of giving up a day to lecture at State U., a specialist can spend the day taping lectures and have them distributed to all the universities that would like to hear him speak. Even small, isolated institutions can thus obtain the services of world-famous experts. They need only have facilities for playing back the recorded materials. As the cost of recording and of equipment for playing back the results decreases, this kind of lecture system becomes increasingly practical and attractive.

The New Media and
Correspondence Instruction

The new media share many of the advantages of the correspondence method. They are all somewhat more flexible to the needs of the individual student than resident instruction, and they are intended to provide a motivational stimulus as well. They are all capable of instructing an expanding student body because they do not cater to a particular size group but to the individual or (in the case of films and projections) to a practically unlimited group.

Many correspondence instruction suppliers fear the new media as rivals. Because they see that correspondence instruction and the new media share many of the same instructional advantages, they fear that each must rival the other for a share of the instructional market. Not so. Because they have similar characteristics, they can more easily be combined into an integrated program.

CERP concluded Chapter 4 by encouraging suppliers to examine subject matter, student qualifications, and their own operational capabilities before offering a course by correspondence. CERP added that although nearly any subject can be taught in part by correspondence, not all subjects can be taught well in their entirety by the correspondence method. The new media offer exciting possibilities to correspondence suppliers for expanding the instructional potential of the correspondence method.

Integrated-media Instruction

In discussing each of the new media, CERP has pointed out some of the particular uses. The supplier need only adapt these uses to his own instructional offerings to create an integrated-media program of instruction.

In a language course which requires reading and hearing, the supplier should provide correspondence instruction accompanied by audio tapes. The correspondence program might include correspondence lessons on how to speak the language in addition to other traditional materials. It might include programmed lessons to provide self-testing and instant feedback on material learned. The course might also make provisions for an exchange of recorded tapes between the student and the instructor. For example, the supplier might send the student a recorded tape demonstrating certain exercises; the student then would practice the lessons and make a recording to be sent to the instructor for audition and comment.

An art appreciation course by correspondence might include a set of art slides for the student to study. As noted above, several open-circuit television programs already offer correspondence instruction in conjunction with a televised course. This allows the student, without ever leaving his home, to receive feedback from a teacher whom he can watch demonstrate and lecture.

Students may someday be able to plug special typewriters into cable outlets or use other devices in their own homes to receive computer-assisted programmed instruction; at the present time, they must go to special computer centers. Students can take correspondence courses to prepare them for their computer-assisted instruction, however, thereby combining the two instructional methods.

Students in many parts of the world use correspondence instruction in conjunction with resident instruction. In some programs correspondence courses are augmented by special intensified periods in laboratories. Group instruction, in which correspondence students meet periodically with a trained instructor, is used successfully by the Federal Aviation Agency in its Directed (Home) Study Program.[4] This program allows the student to benefit from interaction with a live instructor and with other students without being tied down for long periods of time to a resident center.

Many colleges now permit students to take some courses for credit by correspondence. They frequently provide the student with guidance, with special instruction if he runs into difficulty, and with proctored examinations to test his achievement. The student, if matriculated at a resident college, can use all its facilities and thereby profit from many advantages of both the correspondence and the resident method. The same advantages exist in the supervised correspondence program as inaugurated by Mitchell at Benton Harbor. The student gains all the advantages of direct, personal feedback from every lesson and of carefully prepared correspondence lessons which he can complete more or less at his own rate. At the same time, he has a supervisor available who may be able to help him with problems that arise.

The University of Kansas started an experimental program in 1963 in which a selected group of students take a special freshman English course. The usual lectures are replaced by a correspondence course and a special weekly seminar held by a senior professor in the English department. The students receive more individual feedback from the correspondence work and have a closer relationship with a senior member of the faculty through the seminars than would be possible through large lecture sessions.

The University of Houston has used film to teach trigonometry to students. The student receives a notebook with written lessons to accompany the film. The university awards credit to any student who successfully passes the final examination. Many other universities have similar experimental courses involving some of the principles of both correspondence work and the new media.

The following summary is part of the *Report of the Conference on Newer Media in Correspondence Study* published in 1962. It deals solely with audio media and correspondence instruction, but a similar lengthy list could also be drawn up for visual media.

> Audio media have been used in correspondence study situations [in the following ways]: (1) to introduce the teacher and/or the student by having him use the audio media to record biographical information; (2) recording dramatic presentations to present the flavor of the work; (3) in music appreciation courses to allow the pupil to detect the differences being discussed; (4) as an integral part of the assignment wherein the pupil records on audio media rather than on paper; (5) as a supplementary or enriching vehicle to allow the teacher to elaborate and/or present further explanation of the subject matter he is teaching; (6) as a testing device wherein the pupil is evaluated on his grasp of concepts or principles being taught; (7) to give the pupil a greater feeling of personal participation and involvement by giving him a literal "chance to be heard"; (8) as a summarizing device wherein the teacher can present a capsulized review to the pupil; (9) to bring in new, unusual, outside sources

which wouldn't be available to the pupil without utilization of the audio media; (10) in teaching foreign language pronunciation and enunciation; (11) as Tele-Lectures which allow the teacher to tape his presentation, present it to the "class" and then later have a question and answer period with the "class." The Universities of Omaha and Wisconsin and Stevens College have experimented with this; (12) "one-way" utilization wherein the pupil can only play-back—he can not record for teacher play-back. Since the cost of adding recording mechanism is considered non-prohibitive the general feeling evinced at this workshop was to include both rather than only the one way; (13) in the realm of compressed speech, which allows the teacher to play back the recording at a speed faster than that at which it was recorded. Here, again, problems arise concerning tonal quality, comprehensiveness and wear and tear on the instructor. It was reported that up to thirty minutes of compressed time listening is feasible; more than this becomes tiresome; (14) as a loan to public schools and/or public libraries within the immediate vicinity of the student to assure him that he will have equipment available. Such ventures have ranged all the way from depositing units at the library to outright use of the libraries' equipment. Unfortunately this area has not been explored enough to pass judgment on it; (15) the recording of the regular class sessions which the course writer teaches and the use of these recordings as a guide in developing the correspondence course; (16) pictures with accompanying audio tapes . . . used in the medical field; (17) . . . to encourage the use of tapes by subsidization of audio media courses. The consensus of the subgroups was that too few institutions have done this; finally, (18) . . . to avoid dry, boring presentations by using dramatizations, music and conversations involving important personalities. If one will only let his imagination soar, it becomes evident that audio media, in this person's mind, can be used effectively to enliven, encourage and inspire students in any course. Is this not the case?

The following quotation best exemplifies the opinion of the participants at this workshop concerning current uses of the audio media in correspondence study: "People should not try to replace reading by the audio method, nor the audio method by reading. They both have a definite place in correspondence study. They both should be used to supplement the other."[5]

The Systems Approach

The managerial technique of systems analysis has been adapted with encouraging results to the task of meeting instructional problems. Traditionally each instructional tool has been treated as a separate component, independent of other methods and media. The systems approach emphasizes the complexity of instruction and the interdependency of all the components in an instructional system. Instead of trying to solve each problem with a single teaching method, the systems approach pools the available resources for an all-out assault on the interrelated problems of instruction.

With a systems approach a comprehensive program could be developed to provide a variety of educational opportunities for those outside the formal system. Through universities, colleges, public schools, or community centers an external program of education might be offered. Students might find themselves taking a course through some combination of correspondence instruction and programmed instruction, plus attendance at seminars and laboratories, watching video tapes on a television screen, or having individual conferences with their instructors.

This work might be coordinated with work offered on the

campus of an educational institution, public or private, such as a university, college, high school, or junior college. An interesting prospect is for satellite campuses of universities and local junior and community colleges to serve as coordinating centers for a variety of off-campus educational work, such as correspondence instruction. Their facilities could be used to supplement and support the work of students enrolled in off-campus programs.

It is important to emphasize that the systems approach is not a set pattern, or instructional technique, but a means of analyzing an instructional problem and determining a solution. As the solution frequently combines various instructional methods, correspondence instruction is likely to be called upon. The correspondence method may play an especially important role. As the systems approach provides for an increasing amount of independent study, correspondence methods may prove to be the best means for controlling and unifying the diverse media that make up the selected system.

The New Media Producers

The producers and suppliers of the new media are typically giant corporations. IBM, General Electric, Westinghouse, Ampex, Sony, Kodak, Bell & Howell, and all the major educational publishing firms, to name some of the more prominent companies, are deeply involved in new instructional media. They are not only producing the computers, film loops, tape recorders, and programmed instruction books; they are applying their tremendous resources and technology to research and development of even newer instructional ideas and equipment.

These producers stand to profit handsomely from the sale

and operation of their machines or course materials if they can win widespread acceptance for them. Although they perhaps take little note of correspondence instruction at present, they may simply feel that correspondence suppliers have never shown enough interest in innovation or new media to warrant a serious effort at cooperation.

To the many correspondence suppliers operating on marginal budgets, the cost of buying and shipping tapes or films —not to mention the problem of seeing that the student has a proper recorder or viewer—seems to put many of the new media beyond their means. The supplier views these innovations more as rivals than as parts of a compatible system and prefers to try to survive on his own terms rather than participate in a program that would rely on different media and perhaps ultimately resemble present-day correspondence instruction but slightly.

The correspondence supplier who takes this conservative stand risks professional suicide. Although his position may be sound today, the trend for the future indicates a more diverse approach to instruction. Correspondence instruction will be only one of many methods challenging the traditional resident method, but it will do so without the benefit of the research effort and skills of the powerful organizations that will be major suppliers of instruction through the new media. The largest independent correspondence supplier is a midget compared with these titans. The government, seeking to improve the country's educational system, is likely to turn more and more toward the progressive suppliers who are contributing their own time and money to educational research. To grow and prosper, correspondence suppliers must be prepared to change and accept the challenge of the new media.

THE NEED FOR COOPERATION

Correspondence instruction suppliers cannot ignore progress nor can they fully participate in it as long as they distrust one another and refuse to cooperate to meet mutual needs. Common interest dictates cooperation among suppliers, but years of mutual distrust between universities and private home study schools have erected serious barriers to the kinds of programs that are needed.

The seeds of cooperation exist in supplier organizations operating today. But these organizations typically serve the narrow interests of a particular supplier group. To compete with the electronics, communications, and publishing titans, the correspondence suppliers must pool all their resources. They need to sponsor research, eliminate wasteful duplication in their own output, and help train teachers and staff members familiar with the particular advantages and problems of correspondence instruction. Suppliers must also collectively redirect their attention to the enormous problems of accreditation and regulation. Then they can meaningfully begin to improve the image and popular appeal of the correspondence method of instruction.

CERP suggests that suppliers cut across institutional lines to form effective groups for improving the correspondence method and helping it keep pace with instructional innovation. Although such a program is of interest and importance to all correspondence suppliers, CERP points out the special roles that naturally fall to the colleges and universities and to the private home study schools. The colleges and universities, as leaders in instruction, have the knowledge and skills to lead in redirecting the energies of correspondence suppliers toward research and improvement. Private home study groups have the financial resources and the marketing experience to support many of the programs CERP recommends. If the traditional distrust between these two groups of suppliers can be overcome, correspondence instruction can take a decisive step toward meeting many of its most severe problems.

Existing Organizations

Throughout this report, CERP has mentioned many of the different organizations that deal with correspondence supplier problems. These organizations constitute a base upon which supplier cooperation can be built. CERP briefly views the more important of these organizations, not only to record their present activities, but to determine their potential roles in implementing supplier cooperation.

NATIONAL UNIVERSITY EXTENSION ASSOCIATION (NUEA) The NUEA was founded in 1915 to promote and encourage the development of university extension programs. Although correspondence instruction was a major concern of the NUEA from the outset, the establishment of the Division of Correspondence Study in 1955 reconfirmed its importance within the complex of university extension studies.

The Division of Correspondence Study publishes no professional journal and has apparently abandoned its *Newsletter*, once an effective medium for communicating professional opinions and developments. However, in 1962 the division did publish a self-evaluation guide for NUEA correspondence departments entitled *Criteria and Standards*. The division also sponsors the publication A *Guide to Correspondence Study in Colleges and Universities,* providing a list of available correspondence programs and courses. The *Guide* indicates the programs offered by each of the sixty-four colleges or universities in the NUEA with correspondence departments. The publication of the *Guide* represents a major step in cooperation among college and university suppliers, for they were unwilling to exchange syllabi or course information only a few years before. The division's Committee on Research also published the comprehensive *Annotated Bibliography of Correspondence Study, 1897–1960,* a valuable research tool. Furthermore, the NUEA *Proceedings,* extending over more than fifty years, provides facts and records of the growth of university correspondence instruction.

The NUEA and its Division of Correspondence Study are not accrediting agencies. However, they do cooperate with the six regional associations of the National Commission on Accrediting to raise the standards of university correspondence programs. The NUEA holds an annual convention which serves as a forum for discussion of university extension problems and activities and which has been the inspiration for much of the change in university correspondence instruction practices.

Much of the actual innovation has been the work of individual universities or programs within the NUEA. The names of Gayle B. Childs and Knute O. Broady at Nebraska, Charles A. Wedemeyer at Wisconsin, Alice Rowbotham at California, F. Lloyd Hansen at Minnesota, and John L. Davies at Iowa stand out as a few of the important leaders at the university level. Important contributions to literature about the correspondence method have been written by Alfred Hall-Quest, *The University Afield* (a 1926 study sponsored by the Carnegie

Corporation of New York which examined university extension courses and touched briefly on correspondence programs); Walton S. Bittner and Hervey F. Mallory, *University Teaching by Mail* (a comprehensive study made in 1932 of university correspondence departments); Gayle B. Childs and Charles A. Wedemeyer, *New Perspectives in University Correspondence Study* (a 1961 survey that provides the first extensive look at correspondence instruction since Bittner and Mallory's book published twenty-eight years earlier). A new series of considerable importance is *The Brandenburg Memorial Essays*, which grew out of the Brandenburg seminars on correspondence instruction held at the University of Wisconsin. Volumes I and II, edited by Wedemeyer, appeared in 1963 and 1966 respectively.

NATIONAL HOME STUDY COUNCIL (NHSC) John S. Noffsinger, by his strong recommendation in *Correspondence Schools, Lyceums, Chautauquas* (see above, page 111), sparked the creation of the National Home Study Council in 1926. The charter members set out to establish ethical business standards and higher educational standards among private correspondence schools. In doing so, they expected to gain acceptance for their schools as reputable suppliers of correspondence instruction and safeguard them against blanket criticism of all private home study schools as irresponsible or fraudulent operations.

Unlike the NUEA, the NHSC does carry out an accrediting function. Based on its *Documents and Instructions of the Accrediting Commission*, the NHSC's Accrediting Commission considers applications for accreditation from private home study schools. The U.S. Office of Education has recognized the commission as the national accrediting agency for private home study correspondence schools.

The NHSC holds an annual conference to discuss the problems of private correspondence suppliers. Between conferences suppliers meet in workshops to attack precise problems, frequently dealing with advertising, public relations, or other topics of particular import to the supplier who hopes to make a profit from his operation. Forty years ago the major private home study schools were reluctant to share any information at all with competitors; today they are becoming increasingly accustomed and even eager to discuss their problems and experiences. The NHSC has done much to foster cooperation among the private or proprietary suppliers.

The NHSC sponsors three important publications. *The Directory of Accredited Private Home Study Schools* provides a list of NHSC accredited schools and available courses. Many schools that were previously unwilling to cooperate on such a directory have come to accept the value of cross-referral from one school to another. This directory is an important guide for the student, especially as many of them are required (by employers, organizations, etc.) to enroll in NHSC accredited courses.

The *NHSC News*, a monthly trade paper, carries news items on correspondence study and activities of member schools and NHSC committees. *The Home Study Review*, published quarterly, carries no advertising and must be subsidized heavily by the NHSC. The editorial board seeks articles, reports, and comments from international authorities on correspondence instruction. The continual improvement of the *Review* since its first issue in 1960 indicates the intent of the editors to provide a forum for discussion of the problems of correspondence instruction beyond the membership of the NHSC. Although university authorities have contributed articles to the *Review*, the NUEA Division of Correspondence

Study has never accepted a long-standing invitation to serve on the editorial board.

OTHER ORGANIZATIONS AND PUBLICATIONS CERP has already mentioned (see above, pages 113–114) the Commission on Accreditation of Service Experiences (CASE). As the authority on correspondence instruction in the Armed Forces, CASE is the logical organization to represent the military in any joint efforts for supplier cooperation. As the Armed Forces turn more of their enormous resources toward research and experimentation in correspondence instruction, other suppliers are going to look to CASE or some similar organization to share in cooperative efforts to encourage change and rapid development. Colonel Russell V. Ritchey claims: "The military services have today the greatest potential for developing and validating the role of correspondence education."[6] Other suppliers will want to share in some of the benefits as this potential becomes reality. CASE has produced two major publications: *Guide to the Evaluation of Educational Experiences in the Armed Forces* and *Accreditation Policies of State Departments of Education for the Evaluation of Service Experiences and USAFI Examinations*.

CASE was created by the American Council on Education (ACE), which has been active in correspondence instruction in its own right. ACE commissioned Dr. W. W. Charters to write *Opportunities for the Continuing of Education in the Armed Forces*, an evaluative study of USAFI courses, which appeared in 1951. In 1956, ACE published *A Study of the General Educational Development Testing Program*.

The American Council on Education holds an advantageous position for performing an important role in encouraging interinstitutional supplier cooperation. ACE actively encourages research and professional improvement in correspondence instruction. It has the respect of the suppliers and therefore the potential to act as a unifying body and organizer of interinstitutional supplier groups.

The U.S. Office of Education (USOE) now has the authority to recognize accrediting agencies (see above, page 112). It also has the stature and position needed to overcome supplier rivalries and channel supplier energies into the more productive task of preparing for the future. The USOE now operates a Division of Adult Education, but it has no specific subdivision to handle the problems of correspondence instruction. Such a subdivision would be a natural focal point for interinstitutional supplier cooperation and would take the responsibility for such cooperation out of the hands of existing partisan groups which must negotiate for every step they wish to take.

Some of the educational journals publish articles about correspondence instruction, and a few have published special issues devoted to the subject. Among the prominent journals which have thus recognized the importance of correspondence instruction are the *Phi Delta Kappan,* December, 1939; *The Bulletin of the National Association of Secondary-School Principals,* December, 1952; and *The Journal of Experimental Education,* Fall, 1963. Such publications reflect an awareness of the significance of the correspondence method and a growing professionalism among its advocates.

Perhaps the most important of the existing mechanisms for supplier cooperation is the International Council on Correspondence Education (ICCE), which meets approximately every four years to provide an international exchange of views, opinions, and experimental results. Since 1938 the ICCE has met seven times in different countries, and United States correspondence administrators were fairly well represented at the first six meetings. The ICCE *Proceedings,* a valuable source of correspondence instruction information, records details of conference activities. However, CERP recognizes that the ICCE will remain severely limited in its impact so long as such a small percentage of those engaged in correspondence instruction are actually represented at the conference. Attendance, as indicated by the following statistics, took a marked jump at the Seventh Conference. ICCE advocates hope this indicates a trend toward greater participation in future conferences and an increased willingness by suppliers to cooperate on problems and developments.

CONFER-ENCE NO.	AT-TENDANCE	YEAR	NO. OF COUNTRIES REPRE-SENTED	LOCATION
1	88	1938	3	Victoria, B. C., Canada
2	118	1948	6	Lincoln, Nebraska
3	79	1950	3	Christchurch, New Zealand
4	73	1953	8	State College, Pennsylvania
5	76	1957	5	Banff, Alberta, Canada
6	77	1961	5	Gearhart, Oregon
7	225	1965	31	Stockholm, Sweden

Obstacles to Greater Cooperation

The most serious obstacle to greater cooperation, as implied earlier, is the distrust between the university suppliers of correspondence instruction and the private home study schools. The NUEA has been largely unwilling to cooperate with the NHSC for fear that cooperation would be misconstrued as approval or even some form of accreditation. University correspondence administrators have generally felt that private home study schools are too profit-oriented and too little interested in supplying quality instruction.

Although such criticisms were undoubtedly true in the early days of correspondence instruction and may still have some relevance today, CERP feels that the NHSC has come a long way in raising the standards and objectives of the private home study schools. Continued refusal by the universities to cooperate with these suppliers, who are statistically more important than any others except the military, can only serve to retard the improvement of the correspondence method and its acceptance by society.

The critical attitude of university correspondence administrators is typified in this comment by Chester Allen:

> Even a casual study of the operation of the commercial correspondence study schools during the first half century of their operation indicates clearly the hazards to any reputable educational institution making an effort to interchange ideas with them, or their agent, the National Home Study Council. . . . It would seem wise to keep the two types of organizations—the profit seeking commercial correspondence-study schools and the publicly supported University Extension service—completely separate.[7]

One year earlier (1948), at the Second Conference of the ICCE, the formation of a U.S. Association of Correspondence Education to include both private home study schools and university correspondence departments was suggested.[8] The NUEA, in agreeing with Allen's estimate, subsequently turned down the proposal at its thirty-fourth annual meeting in 1949 because, "In such an organization the proprietary schools would get prestige from us, while we would get nothing from them."[9]

Again in 1954, the NUEA Committee on Relations between the NUEA and the National Home Study Council "was unanimous in expressing its concern over problems involved in any possible official recognition of the National Home Study Council, lest it imply accreditation status."[10]

However, a thaw seems to have begun. At the Seventh Conference of the ICCE, held in Stockholm in 1965, the question of NUEA and NHSC cooperation arose. Although it received no affirmative response from university representatives, the usual harsh criticisms of proprietary schools were absent. The answer volunteered to the question used general terms and avoided the basic issues, perhaps indicating an unwillingness to take the kind of intractable position that previously characterized any attempts at reconciliation of the two groups.[11] Further evidence is offered by this constructive and optimistic statement from Charles Wedemeyer in 1964:

> Each passing year shows a closer relationship between NUEA and NHSC. The schism should be closed but probably there should not be too close a relationship. NHSC shows evidence of becoming a good organization. There are more areas in which it and NUEA can work together than there are areas of disagreement.[12]

CERP has indicated that this schism must be closed for the benefit of all correspondence suppliers. The time is propitious. CERP suggests that the American Council on Education initiate the formation of a cooperative supplier organization. ACE has the needed prestige and the interest in the health and effectiveness of correspondence instruction. Although the NUEA seems to be softening considerably in its opposition to cooperation with the NHSC, CERP feels that the stimulus of some respected outside organization working for greater cooperation will help overcome the reluctance to reversing a traditional attitude. ACE could supervise such a cooperative group until it could stand by itself and ensure a continuing effort at cooperation.

CERP also recommends that the U.S. Office of Education play a greater role in correspondence instruction. At present, the recognition of accrediting bodies is the sole supervisory function of the USOE in correspondence instruction. CERP would like to see the USOE establish a home study office or at least a home study desk within the Division of Adult Education. The USOE cannot ignore the importance of correspondence instruction, and it could be instrumental in fostering improvements in the method and its operation. Through such involvement, the USOE could eventually become a much more effective regulating body, preventing and punishing abuses, than the Federal Trade Commission, courts, or Post Office Department can be.

Although supplier cooperation may come in time, the need is great at present. Interested groups should be encouraged to stimulate cooperative attitudes and set up agencies for cooperation as quickly as possible. Other instructional methods are experimenting in new media and new instructional techniques; the correspondence method is dragging its heels. For their own survival, suppliers must reconsider old rivalries and look ahead to new cooperative relationships.

GOALS OF COOPERATION

CERP has emphasized the need for cooperation, but such emphasis is meaningless unless attached to specified goals. Once the suppliers agree to cooperate, once the cooperating agencies have been established, they must have goals toward which they can work.

CERP believes that the special characteristics of correspondence instruction and the special problems suppliers now face indicate two sets of goals cooperative efforts can aim for: (1) research and instructional goals and (2) accreditation and regulation goals. If instruction changes appreciably, accreditation standards and procedures will have to be modified. Therefore, CERP treats research and instructional goals first and follows with an examination of the goals for cooperation in accrediting.

Research and Instructional Goals

CERP recognizes five distinct goals for cooperation in instruction and research: (1) economy of effort, (2) cooperative external facilities, (3) teacher training, (4) cooperative research units, and (5) a national examining university. Each of these five goals has been carefully selected for its relevance to priority problems now facing suppliers of correspondence instruction.

ECONOMY OF EFFORT   CERP has repeatedly indicated that scarcity of resources is one of the correspondence supplier's most severe problems. While recognizing this, suppliers have shown themselves to be nevertheless unwilling to pool their resources to eliminate wasteful expense and activity. Instead of trying to list every example of wasteful behavior on the part of correspondence suppliers, CERP offers a single case as a model: the duplication of courses. There are approximately fifteen thousand correspondence courses available to correspondence students. Universities and colleges alone have prepared and serviced about nine thousand of these courses.

Every correspondence program or school that wishes to offer a course in a particular subject—accounting for example —must hire a course writer to create it. He will have his own knowledge of the subject as a starting point and access to a certain amount of reference material. He may be chosen for his knowledge or for his skill as a course writer. He may actually be the best person to write such a course.

However, it would be totally unrealistic to imagine that every correspondence program could produce such a qualified best person to write each of its courses. Many programs, especially those with the most severe financial limitations, may be forced to offer courses of mediocre or inferior quality. Then the program suffers, and the students suffer as well.

Even if the ideal were possible and every program could have first-class writers, the duplication of effort would be wasteful. CERP recognizes the need for different kinds of courses to meet the needs of different students. CERP also realizes that a certain amount of competition and freedom to choose between courses is important. But there is no need for more than 130 different correspondence programs to offer accounting courses. Such an expenditure of effort and resources represents a sizable waste.

No one considers it strange that teachers no longer prepare their own textbooks. Textbooks are published commercially, and the teacher or the institution selects the one that best meets the needs of the students and the course. CERP suggests that correspondence courses could also be prepared and marketed commercially. This would give even the poorest school the opportunity to provide courses created by experts. The schools could alter courses and presumably would create their own whenever they chose to meet an unusual demand. Most programs would be able to improve the quality of the courses they offer, and the commercial competition would hopefully stimulate continual improvement.

Programs that now create their own courses at a profit or that are entirely content with their present operation are unlikely to embrace the idea of commercial publication of correspondence programs. Others may actually fear that commercial publication will limit their ability to experiment or to offer courses with little popular appeal. Although the latter argument seems to have little basis in fact (CERP is not suggesting that *all* courses be created for commercial publication), CERP recognizes that there may be considerable opposition to the proposal. However, the advantages in economy and quality to be gained for correspondence instruction make commercial publication of correspondence courses worth serious consideration.

COOPERATIVE EXTERNAL FACILITIES By *external facilities* CERP means such facilities as are necessary for proper instruction and are normally found in resident centers of instruction. Often correspondence students must do without these facilities entirely. Students and suppliers are both greatly limited by the lack of such facilities, and a scheme to make them available would greatly expand the possibilities of the correspondence method.

Scientific laboratories stand out as a prime example. Many correspondence suppliers now offer largely theoretical science courses. If correspondence students had access to extension laboratories or some kind of special laboratory center where they could complete experiments, the correspondence method could greatly increase its effectiveness in teaching science.

Language laboratories, libraries, and other facilities normally identified with resident institutions could be coordinated with scientific laboratories in extension centers.

Participating suppliers, including state and federal governments, could finance their construction and operation. Such centers could be placed in areas of greatest need where most students would be able to get to them. Because of the flexibility of correspondence instruction, students could concentrate all their laboratory work into a short period of time or spread it out to be completed at their own convenience.

Such facilities would go a long way toward silencing the criticism of correspondence instruction as too dependent on the written word. Although opposition might arise because of the cost or because such a change would really "make correspondence instruction into something entirely different," the possibilities for expanded and improved instruction make such extension centers seem very attractive.

TEACHER TRAINING No instructional method (remember, CERP defines instruction to include student-instructor interaction) can function properly without trained instructors. CERP has already pointed out the unfortunate lack of courses to prepare instructors for the task of teaching by correspondence. Most teachers complete their training without ever coming into direct contact with the correspondence method, either as students or as future instructors.

Thus each program must try to train its own instructors or merely leave them to their own devices. Proper training by individual suppliers would be costly and time consuming. CERP suggests that suppliers pool their resources and their influence and either set up special training courses themselves or persuade colleges of education to undertake the task of preparing correspondence instructors. The quality of the instruction a student receives depends in part on the ability of his instructor. One of the best ways to improve the quality of a correspondence program is to obtain and train competent instructors. As the suppliers have insufficient resources and cannot exert enough pressure alone, CERP encourages them to cooperate to provide programs for training correspondence instructors. It is not unreasonable, furthermore, to suggest that such courses could adequately be taught at least in part by correspondence.

COOPERATIVE RESEARCH UNITS The massive communications and electronics concerns are pouring time and money into instructional research. Not even the largest of correspondence suppliers can hope to compete with them, although the military and the federal government could if they took a direct interest. In order to produce a research effort commensurate with the task of keeping correspondence instruction up to date with the new developments in education, all suppliers must cooperate.

CERP suggests that the various suppliers agree to establish a correspondence research foundation. The universities have the research know-how; the private home study schools, the government, and interested corporations have the necessary financial resources. They should be put to work in a cooperative venture that would benefit all concerned by improving the method. The foundation should operate independently, thus freeing itself from any bias that might lead to conflict or claims of unfairness. By its independence, it would also stand to acquire a larger portion of the multibillion dollar investment made annually in education and educational research in the United States.

A NATIONAL EXAMINING UNIVERSITY CERP feels strongly that correspondence instruction cannot expect to attain parity in the public mind with traditional forms of instruction until a means is found of validating the educational level and the course experience of the external student, i.e., one outside the formal system. This is a practical problem for the external student who needs the validation for purposes of employment, promotion, certification, license, or entrance to college.

CERP recommends that a national examining university be organized and have among its functions the establishment of standards for informal courses, accreditation of courses, and the testing and validating of educational experience (however gained) in terms of units, credits, or some other measure acceptable to the academic world and in keeping with our educational tradition. The idea for a university of this nature has precedent. For more than 130 years the University of London has served as an external examining body which, as it states in its information bulletin, "within the relatively narrow limits of its activities, . . . acquired a great reputation and influenced the development of national education in many ways."[13]

The American Council on Education and the National Commission on Accrediting are logical sponsors to launch the national examining university. The former through its Commission on Accreditation of Service Experiences is already involved in the General Educational Development testing program. The sponsors could call upon the experiences of others such as the NHSC Accrediting Commission and the Council on College-Level Examinations of the College Entrance Examination Board.

The national examining university could be empowered to certify the educational level of the individual and his competence in a particular subject or field. It could be authorized to issue high school equivalency certificates and to grant degrees from the associate level to graduate work.

Although some suppliers might suffer because their courses

are not of the quality to prepare students to meet examination requirements, correspondence suppliers in general would profit enormously. A national examining university would engender respect for correspondence instruction in cases in which many now criticize correspondence courses because they seem too slack. The national examining university examinations would be trustworthy, and academic bodies would be much less reluctant to award or accept credit for courses taken by correspondence. With the establishment of such an examining body, correspondence instruction would take a large step toward the recognition and respect it so eagerly seeks.

Note: In 1963, the Big Ten universities plus the University of Chicago started to explore the possibilities of offering regional correspondence courses. The text of the report of the 1963 Conference on Inter-Institutional Cooperation is reproduced in the notes because it considers many of the themes relevant to the broader questions of supplier cooperation.[14] The recommendations made at the conference were not translated into formal action but are indicative of the problems considered.

Accreditation and Regulation Goals

CERP has pointed out that gaining acceptance for correspondence instruction is one of the suppliers' greatest tasks. To improve the image of correspondence instruction and gain greater respect for it as an instructional method, suppliers have created mechanisms for voluntary accreditation.

In order to minimize government regulation, these suppliers also perform a certain amount of self-policing. But a full-scale cooperative effort at establishing acceptable standards and adhering to them would greatly further the cause of correspondence instruction to the advantage of all who use the method with integrity. CERP suggests that suppliers cooperate to (1) establish a set of standards, (2) submit to accreditation procedures based on those standards, and (3) thereby establish a logical mechanism for self-regulation.

ACCEPTABLE STANDARDS There are at present no uniform standards for correspondence instruction programs. Correspondence divisions in universities are sheltered under the general accreditation of the institution; the NHSC has its own criteria for judging applicant schools. Some schools do not seek any form of accreditation and meet no standards but their own. Unfortunately, all correspondence programs suffer by association from the reputations of the worst. If a supplier could show that he has satisfied the requirements of a rigorous set of standards established by some respectable independent organization, he could verify the merit of his program.

Such a set of standards would perform a second important function for correspondence suppliers. High standards on an industrywide basis would encourage an upgrading of the entire correspondence process. Suppliers would have a specific goal at which to aim their improvements. Inadequate programs would have their deficiencies judged and pointed out according to standards known to all. A set of standards would provide an excellent stimulus to the improvement of correspondence instruction.

ACCREDITATION A national examining university of the type suggested could certainly establish the accrediting apparatus to evaluate programs and courses.

Another approach to satisfying the special evaluation and accrediting needs of correspondence instruction would be through existing agencies. The basic structure for accrediting exists in the NHSC Accrediting Commission. If the Accrediting Commission were to be completely separated from NHSC and recognized by the National Commission on Accrediting as an independent accrediting agency for correspondence instruction, it could serve the purpose of general accreditation. In the case of colleges and universities, it would work through the six regional associations.

Such a body would be responsible for developing, in cooperation with supplier groups to be served, a set of standards to be used as criteria for accreditation and for judging whether a particular institution lives up to those standards. An institution would receive accreditation on its own merits irrespective of whether it operates for a profit or as part of a university extension department.

Of course, institutions that advertise and recruit students would be judged on the honesty and fairness of their recruiting practices as well as on their instructional procedures. Standards would be applied whenever appropriate to the individual institution. Yet this should pose no additional hardship to any institution; each will merely be judged on its own merits.

CERP again suggests that the American Council on Education and the National Commission on Accrediting lead the way in bringing the several institutions and agencies together to explore means for establishing the accrediting and evaluating services so needed in correspondence instruction. This is not a criticism of the NUEA or the NHSC which now perform an important function by encouraging improvement in programs of member universities and schools.

CERP feels that an independent accrediting body would produce advantages for all and make clear to the public the merit of accredited institutions. Furthermore, academic institutions would be more likely to accept transfer credit gained through correspondence instruction, and the general public would be happier knowing that it could choose a correspondence program that had met an accepted standard of quality.

The lowly status of correspondence instruction on college and university campuses is some indication it is not receiving the attention it deserves from accrediting authorities. In CERP's judgment this should receive the attention of the Federation of Regional Accrediting Commissions of Higher Education. The federation, which coordinates the policies and planning of the six regional associations, is responsible for codifying and developing " 'general principles and procedures for institutional evaluation and accreditation' toward the establishment of a 'national consensus for regional application.' "[15]

CERP has pointed out the social need for general accrediting of institutions offering correspondence instruction. There is also a need for specific (professional) accrediting of correspondence programs in professional fields, as for example, in engineering. This should be the responsibility of the professional accrediting associations. The National Commission on Accrediting should encourage the professional associations which it has recognized to broaden their coverage to include validation of professional courses and programs taught by correspondence.

CERP believes that if accrediting is to have meaning in the future there should be a national voluntary organization, i.e., one not under government control, empowered to recognize and coordinate the accrediting activities of all agencies in fields in which accrediting serves the public interest. Seemingly, the colleges and universities standing at the educational pinnacle should be willing to provide leadership and impetus for organizing a voluntary group of this nature. Actually, this could be accomplished through a redefining of the function and broadening of the organization and scope of the National Commission on Accrediting. For example, NCA could be organized as a system of divisions which would include a division for higher education, another for secondary schools, and a third for trade, technical, and home study schools. NCA then, in truth, would be a national commission concerned with issues of accrediting. Such an organization would obviate the need for the U.S. Office of Education to become increasingly involved in matters of accrediting each time a new federal program of aid to education is enacted.

If the universities and colleges are unwilling to meet this responsibility to education, it is to be hoped that a parallel voluntary organization will emerge along the lines of NCA to meet the need for monitoring and coordinating efforts of accrediting agencies not covered by NCA. The alternative would appear to be a further extension of federal evaluation of educational quality.

REGULATION CERP has continually stressed the value of self-regulation. The government agencies can do only a partial job at best. The best way to regulate the quality of correspondence programs and to protect honest suppliers from the unfair claims and practices of fraudulent operators is to exert collective pressure on the latter from within the industry.

Self-regulation alone, however, will not eliminate the frauds and the cheats. It thus behooves the several states and the federal agencies to continue their regulatory efforts. The prime responsibility lies with the states. The fact that approximately half the states have taken no steps to regulate correspondence schools does not mean that they are not a proper instrumentality to do so. It would seem reasonable that states consider the necessary measures within their policing power to protect their citizens.

Both the Federal Trade Commission and the U.S. Post Office Department would agree that the most effective day-to-day regulation of fraudulent schools could be achieved through state legislation and enforcement. However, both of these federal agencies are cognizant of their responsibilities and would welcome the personnel and resources that would make them more potent forces in curbing the unethical and illegal practices of correspondence schools. It is in the public interest that both state and federal agencies be provided with the authority and resources necessary to regulate the private home study school industry.

PLANNING FOR THE FUTURE

There remain certain tasks for the supplier which are not necessarily linked to present problems or to encouraging supplier cooperation. These are the problems of planning for the future and of being prepared to meet future problems. The supplier cannot always predict future problems, but he can prepare himself to deal with them as they arise.

Instruction and instructional techniques are the focus of governmental and scholarly attention at this time as they have never been before. Instruction is changing rapidly, and correspondence suppliers must be thinking of the future now or risk being left behind.

Specifying the Role of Correspondence Instruction

The role of correspondence instruction in present-day society is an ambiguous one. If the correspondence method is to grow and win a fair share of the instructional task of the future, correspondence administrators must begin to determine just what the future role of the method is to be. Will correspondence instruction be able to go it alone? Or will new media force the correspondence method to combine with different instructional methods?

Although administrators may not be able to answer such questions now, they must begin to think about them if correspondence instruction is to meet its potential. The more clearly administrators determine their objectives for the future, the more successful suppliers are likely to be in attaining them.

Systems Approach

CERP recommends that all suppliers consider taking a systems approach to meeting the instructional needs of their students. The challenge of multimedia demands a response that is flexible and adapted to the particular needs of each instructional problem. No method that cannot change to meet the specific needs of its users is likely to survive at a time when specialization is increasing.

The systems approach may eventually dictate not only cooperation among correspondence suppliers but cooperation with suppliers of different methods of instruction as well. If the result is a better instructional method, correspondence suppliers cannot afford to ignore it.

Keeping Ahead

Correspondence suppliers should begin considering the population explosion and the changes in the structure of knowledge. Both will have profound influence on the shape of instruction in the future. Those suppliers who are prepared to meet the rapidly changing demands on instruction will have a decided advantage over those who try to meet the problems only after they can no longer ignore them.

Suppliers are advised to give considerable attention to long-range planning. If the suppliers wait for the demand to reach a level at which the course becomes economically feasible, they may be too late: another instructional method may already have captured the young market. Only by planning ahead can the correspondence supplier hope to keep ahead.

Constant Improvement

Maintaining the status quo in a changing environment may mean suffering an actual decline. Suppliers must make some progress just to keep up with increasing demands and changing patterns of instruction. Even if a set of standards is established for all suppliers by an independent accrediting body, those standards must not remain static. They must be continually upgraded as a stimulus to constant improvement.

Only by constantly improving the standard of instruction and by controlling the standard of business practices among correspondence suppliers can the correspondence method hope to win the respect of the public and acquire a full share of the expanding instructional market.

CONCLUSION

Correspondence instruction does have an important role to play in providing instruction to a population with varied demands and varied capabilities. Yet the role is neither automatic nor assured. Correspondence suppliers must take up the challenge of changing to meet new demands. In addressing the White House Conference on Education in July, 1965, Dr. John W. Gardner pointed out:

> The toughest question facing us now, in my judgment, is whether we have the courage and flexibility and imagination to innovate as the times require. Let us not deceive ourselves. The old ways of doing things are not good enough. But giving up the old ways will be painful. Institutions fear change. In the face of change we all grow defensive, we all move toward protecting our particular vested interests. But the overriding vested interest of all of us is in the vitality of American education. That is the precious thing that we hold in trust.[16]

CERP has accepted the challenge of trying to give specific direction to the change Dr. Gardner invokes. CERP concludes this report with a statement of recommendations offered in the spirit of constructive advice and in the hope that they will receive thoughtful consideration from those who care about correspondence instruction, its present operation, and its future improvement.

RECOMMENDATIONS

A. Correspondence instruction should be integrated into the educational effort of the United States.
   1. The U. S. Office of Education should establish a home study office in its Division of Adult Education.
   2. The nationwide Compact for Education through its Educational Commission of the States is urged to include correspondence instruction in its thinking in exploring

ways in which it may achieve the educational objectives of the several states.

3. Educational planners within the several states should study the role which correspondence instruction could effectively play as a component of an integrated system of secondary and higher education on a statewide basis.

4. Colleges of education should consider the need to train teachers in the techniques of correspondence instruction. They are urged to incorporate problems pertinent to correspondence instruction in their research investigations.

B. All suppliers of correspondence instruction should consider taking a systems approach toward meeting their educational objectives, evaluating other instructional methods and media as well as correspondence instruction, and using that combination which best achieves educational objectives within a feasible cost structure.

C. A basis should be established for joint action on the part of all supplier systems to deal with the many problems confronting correspondence instruction. CERP suggests that the American Council on Education take the initiative in assembling a group of supplier representatives and in assisting the group to form an ongoing arrangement for joint action.

D. An independent research foundation should be established to undertake the research urgently needed in the field of correspondence instruction. The foundation could be financially supported by private home study schools, business organizations which expect to profit from the multibillion dollar annual investment in education, universities, governmental agencies, and nonprofit foundations.

E. The excessive and uneconomical course duplication should be reduced, thereby freeing resources to provide better courses, more frequent updating of courses, and better teaching. CERP suggests this could be accomplished:

1. By having committees of the Division of Correspondence Study of the National University Extension Association agree upon the most appropriate schools to prepare particular courses and make them available, on a basis to be determined, to other suppliers.
2. By having regional university groups arrange to provide both high-risk courses and bread-and-butter courses on a regional basis.
3. By utilizing commercially published courses prepared by recognized subject-matter specialists. This arrangement could effectively serve other institutional areas as well as universities.

F. Since universities occupy a position at the pinnacle of American education, it is of critical importance that their programs be of the best quality. Therefore, a university which cannot or will not make a quality investment in its correspondence instruction department is urged to close its correspondence study operation.

G. A national examining university should be established to validate the educational experiences of the external student and to grant degrees. CERP suggests that such a university be sponsored by organizations of impeccable reputation such as the American Council on Education and the National Commission on Accrediting.

H. Because of the great variation in the quality of correspondence courses, it is essential that a means be provided for independent accreditation of programs and institutions offering work through correspondence instruction. The American Council on Education and the National Commission on Accrediting should take the responsibility for assembling representatives of the several agencies involved to explore ways in which this could be accomplished. CERP suggests alternate possibilities:

1. The National Commission on Accrediting could take the leadership in the organization of an independent accrediting agency that would be recognized by the National Commission on Accrediting; possibly the Accrediting Commission of the National Home Study Council could be separated from the council and reorganized into such an independent accrediting agency.

2. The responsibility of existing accrediting agencies could be broadened:

   a. The Federation of Regional Accrediting Commissions of Higher Education should consider the responsibilities of regional associations in examining correspondence instruction programs of colleges and universities and recommend procedures through which the regional associations can meet their responsibilities.

   b. The National Commission on Accrediting should encourage recognized professional accrediting associations to assume the responsibility for accrediting professional programs offered by correspondence instruction in private home study schools as well as in colleges and universities; the National Commission on Accrediting could work with professional associations in developing and perfecting procedures.

I. A national voluntary organization should be established to recognize and coordinate accrediting activities of agencies in fields in which accrediting serves the public interest. CERP suggests alternate ways in which this could be accomplished:

1. Redefine the function and broaden the organization and

scope of the National Commission on Accrediting to accomplish the foregoing recommendation.

2. Organize a commission parallel to the National Commission on Accrediting to provide a monitoring service for accrediting agencies not now recognized by the National Commission on Accrediting.

J. The several states and the federal agencies should undertake rigorous regulation of private home study schools to prevent fraudulent operations and deceptive practices.

1. States which currently have laws regulating private home study schools should reexamine these laws to ascertain whether they are accomplishing their objectives. States which have weak regulatory laws or have no legislation regulating home study schools are urged to enact appropriate legislation.

2. The Federal Trade Commission, the U.S. Post Office Department, and regulatory agencies of the several states should be furnished with adequate authority and resources—personnel and budget—to enforce current regulations and prosecute offenders.

NOTES

1. Edward J. Green, *The Learning Process and Programmed Instruction* (New York: Holt, Rinehart and Winston, Inc., 1962).

B. F. Skinner, *Verbal Behavior* (New York: Appleton-Century-Crofts, Inc., 1957).

Wendell I. Smith and J. William Moore (eds.), *Programmed Learning* (Princeton, N.J.: D. Van Nostrand Company, Inc., 1962).

2. *Simulation and Small Business Executive Development,* Bureau of Business Research, The University of Texas, Austin, 1962.

3. Rolf Lundgren talk, *Proceedings, Seventh International Conference, International Council on Correspondence Education,* June 13–17, 1965, pp. 36–37.

4. *The Directed (Home) Study Program in the Federal Aviation Agency,* Federal Aviation Agency Academy, Oklahoma City, Okla., 1962, p. 13.

5. *Report of the Conference on Newer Media in Correspondence Study,* prepared at The University of Texas in cooperation with the U.S. Office of Education, The University of Texas, Division of Extension, Austin, 1962, pp. 36–37.

6. Russell V. Ritchey, "Correspondence Education in the United States Air Force," mimeographed manuscript, Nov. 16, 1965, p. 4.

7. Chester Allen, "Commercial Correspondence Study Schools Private Enterprises for Profit and Some Implications for Public Education of Youth in Wisconsin," Jan. 5, 1949. (Mimeographed.)

8. *Proceedings of the Second International Conference on Correspondence Education,* Oct. 11–15, 1948, p. 32.

9. *Proceedings of the Thirty-fourth Annual Meeting of the National University Extension Association,* May 2–5, 1949, p. 77.

10. *Proceedings of the Thirty-ninth Annual Meeting of the National University Extension Association,* May, 1954, p. 114.

11. *Proceedings, Seventh International Conference, International Council on Correspondence Education,* June 13–17, 1965, p. 123.

12. CERP interviews with Charles A. Wedemeyer, Director, Correspondence Instruction, University of Wisconsin, Aug. 25, 1964.

13. *General Regulations and Information for External Students* (London: University of London, 1960), p. 7.

14. REPORT OF A CONFERENCE ON INTER-INSTITUTIONAL
OF CORRESPONDENCE COURSES, SEPTEMBER 17–18, 1963,
MADISON, WISCONSIN

Main Topics Discussed:
Potential Areas of Cooperation

I. Sharing of costs or other risks in development of "high risk" courses, i.e., relatively expensive, low enrollment courses; courses for which faculty are not available at reasonable cost; courses in new content areas (e.g., the so-called exotic languages, computer technology), etc. Methods of cooperation proposed:

A. Purchase by several CIC institutions of course materials developed by one correspondence study department (assuming competent faculty available for instruction).

B. Sharing of costs of developing a new course or sequence of courses by two or more schools.

C. "Sharing" of faculty; e.g., cooperation of non-correspondence study schools in making available local faculty resources for writing correspondence study courses for other CIC schools.

D. Withdrawal from new high-risk disciplines in which correspondence study programs are already under development at another CIC institution and referral of interested students to that school.

E. Ultimately, perhaps, termination of certain courses by all CIC schools except the one or two whose faculty resources (and other circumstances) are particularly suited for correspondence study programs in that academic discipline, and support (not yet defined) of these courses by all other CIC schools; inventory of correspondence study course duplications now existing among CIC institutions.

The discussion repeatedly stressed the importance of securing appropriate academic approval and cooperation in course planning as a primary base for administrative cooperation.

II. A. Referrals of students by non-correspondence study schools, or correspondence study schools not offering a particular course, to CIC institutions which do offer the course.

   B. Establishment of some apparatus by non-correspondence study schools for handling referrals.

   C. More systematic use of NUEA *Guide to Correspondence Courses*.

III. A. Need for a concerted effort to encourage acceptance of transfer credit for correspondence study courses by those CIC institutions which do not now accept such credit freely (i.e., on same basis as resident class credit).

   B. Problems of excessive limitations on correspondence study credits applicable toward a degree at some schools.

IV. A. Cooperative experiments and research in combining correspondence study with TV, radio, programmed instruction, and other teaching devices.

   B. Cooperation in planning and executing such experiments, in securing grants from government and private agencies to support research, etc.

V. Foreign programs; e.g., translations of courses into foreign languages, development of programs for such agencies as the Peace Corps, AID, Institute for International Education.

VI. Need for some apparatus to facilitate communication among correspondence study departments in CIC schools.

VII. A "consumer's guide" to correspondence study courses which not only lists but evaluates these courses.

Conclusions and recommendations

1. The CIC directorate is urged to bring together the Registrars, Deans of Arts and Sciences, and Correspondence Study Directors of all CIC institutions to consider all problems of credit acceptance for correspondence study courses.
2. The CIC directorate is urged to support a meeting of the Directors of Correspondence Study, Radio-TV, and Audio-Visual Education of all CIC institutions to examine the problems and challenges of multi media instruction.
3. The correspondence study departments of CIC institutions agree to issue a monthly memorandum (on the fifteenth of each month), to inform their colleagues of the following:
   a. correspondence study courses being planned
   b. courses under revision
   c. courses needed but not planned
   d. courses under production
4. A committee is to be named to draft a statement of the criteria which determine the quality of a correspondence course. John Davies of Iowa will chair the committee.
5. The group present will meet again to continue its discussions, expenses to be borne by the participating institutions. Charles A. Wedemeyer and representatives of two other CIC universities will comprise a Report, Agenda, and Time and Place Committee.

Participants gave unanimous support to the above proposals.

15. *Procedures of Regional Associations in Accrediting Institutions of Higher Education* (Washington, D.C.: National Commission on Accrediting, n.d.), p. 4.
16. John W. Gardner, statement, *White House Conference on Education: A Milestone for Educational Progress*, Subcommittee on Education of the Committee on Labor and Public Welfare, U.S. Senate, Washington, D.C., 1965, p. 175.

Methodology

The CERP study was primarily a comprehensive analysis of existing data. A considerable amount of information was collected directly from institutions offering correspondence instruction. Most of the institutions selected for visits and depth interviews were considered to be among the better institutions offering such instruction. The selections were based on consultations held with a number of people well acquainted with correspondence instruction in the United States. At each institution, the depth interview was based on an open-end questionnaire.

A detailed questionnaire was sent to every institution known to offer correspondence work. The total response was approximately 30 percent with most of the better schools responding.

A number of institutions were asked to provide copies of their instructional material. The course materials were then submitted to subject-matter specialists who evaluated the courses following a guideline which CERP provided. Analyses were also made of catalogs of schools offering correspondence instruction.

Several approaches were used in securing information from individuals considered to be experts in areas pertinent to the study. Interviews were conducted with recognized leaders in the correspondence instruction field and with specialists in collateral areas such as adult education, credit by examination, and innovation in educational media and methods. Sixteen staff papers were commissioned as supplemental material; they are listed in Appendix B. CERP initiated considerable correspondence and discussion with officers and committee chairmen of the Division of Correspondence Study of the National University Extension Association and the National Home Study Council. A special survey was made of the members of NUEA's Division of Correspondence Study Administrative Committee and NHSC's Research and Educational Standards Committee.

Illustrative of the range of contacts necessary for a study of this type are the following projects which were among those carried out.

Information was collected from organizations which had closed down their correspondence instruction programs to learn why the programs had been closed. Surveys were made of a number of small business firms to learn what use they made of correspondence instruction. A survey was made of *Fortune*'s 750 largest firms to learn what use they made of correspondence instruction and which ones were teaching by correspondence or using correspondence courses supplied by others—or doing both. A survey was also made of federal agencies and state governments to gather information on their uses of correspondence instruction.

A most interesting aspect of the study was a survey conducted to determine the public attitude toward correspondence instruction. Nationally known people in the United States whose opinions are widely respected and who are representative of a wide range of occupational categories were asked their views on various forms of instruction and on alternative uses for correspondence instruction.

To obtain their opinions, CERP's survey used the semantic differential (developed by Osgood, Suci, and Tannenbaum in *The Measurement of Meaning* and described in detail in that text) which is designed to measure the different components of attitude. A response of approximately 40 percent was received from those surveyed (see Figures 3–1 to 3–3).

When appropriate, limited surveys were made of selected groups to gather information on special aspects of supplier problems and on the uses of correspondence instruction, as for example, a survey of the finances of selected private home study schools and university correspondence departments.

An extensive search of libraries was conducted to find all possible source material on correspondence instruction and related areas. The search included books, magazine and journal articles, monographs, master's theses, and doctoral dissertations.

The authors attended pertinent conferences in the United States, including annual meetings of the Division of Correspondence Study of the National University Extension Association, National Home Study Council, and Association of Home Study Schools.

Information was collected on practices in foreign countries. Interviews were conducted and schools visited in Canada, Europe, and Mexico. The authors attended the Seventh International Conference of the International Council on Correspondence Education held in June, 1965.

After the report was initially prepared, each chapter was sent to two or more reviewers for criticism.

Correspondence Education Research Project

Research Staff

Ossian MacKenzie, Director (The Pennsylvania State University)

Edward L. Christensen, Associate Director (Brigham Young University)

Paul H. Rigby, Associate Director (The Pennsylvania State University)

Kyle MacKenzie, Research Assistant (The Pennsylvania State University)

Marilynn Reese, Research Secretary, 1964–1965 (The Pennsylvania State University)

Staff Papers

Robert Allen (University of Miami), "Home Study and Leisure Time"

Knute O. Broady (University of Alabama), "History of Correspondence Instruction"

Gayle B. Childs (University of Nebraska), "The Role of Correspondence Education in Professional Development"

Burton R. Clark (University of California), "Education in American Society"

Stephen M. Corey (University of Miami; formerly, Columbia University), "The Facilitation of Learning"

John L. Davies (University of Iowa), "Correspondence Study in Formal Education"

Cornelius W. Gillam (University of Pennsylvania), "The Legal Environment of Correspondence Education"

Jacob J. Kaufman (The Pennsylvania State University), "The Role of Correspondence Education in Training and Retraining"

Helen Kempfer (The Graduate School, U. S. Department of Agriculture; formerly, Secretary, Accrediting Commission, National Home Study Council), "The Role of Programmed Learning in Correspondence Education"

Edward S. Lynn (University of Arizona; formerly, Director of Education, American Institute of Certified Public Accountants), "Correspondence Instruction in Professional Development"

Allan O. Pfnister (Wittenberg University), "The Theory of Accrediting and the Applicability of Accrediting to Correspondence Education"

Peter H. Rossi and John W. C. Johnstone (National Opinion Research Center, University of Chicago), "Social Aspects of Correspondence Education"

Carl J. Schaefer (Rutgers—The State University), "The Role of the Correspondence Method in Vocational Education"

John E. Walsh (International Correspondence Schools), "The Role of Correspondence Education in Vocational Training and Retraining"

Charles A. Wedemeyer (University of Wisconsin), "Some Hypotheses Concerning Correspondence Education and Other Instructional Media"

Paul Woodring (Western Washington State College, and Education Editor, *Saturday Review*), "The Education of Innovators"

Consultants

Robert Allen (University of Miami)

Knute O. Broady (University of Alabama)

Gayle B. Childs (University of Nebraska)

Stephen M. Corey (University of Miami; formerly, Columbia University)

Cornelius W. Gillam (University of Pennsylvania)

Edward Hindsman (Indiana University)

A. A. Liveright (Boston University)

Advisers

John L. Davies (University of Iowa)

Lawrence E. Dennis (Chancellor, University of Rhode Island)

Edward C. Estabrooke (American School)

William A. Fowler (National Home Study Council)

David A. Lockmiller (National Home Study Council)

William K. Selden (formerly, National Commission on Accrediting)

Charles A. Wedemeyer (University of Wisconsin)

National Home Study Council, Committee on Research and Educational Standards

National University Extension Association, Administrative Committee of the Division of Correspondence Study

Interviewers (in addition to Research Staff)

Dorothy Cameron (University of British Columbia)
William A. Fowler (National Home Study Council)
Cornelius W. Gillam (University of Pennsylvania)
David A. Leuthold (University of Missouri)
Elizabeth Powell (University of Georgia)
Neel Proctor (University of Missouri at Kansas City)

Course Reviewers

John Alden (Duke University)
Philip Ashby (Princeton University)
J. O. Bailey (University of North Carolina)
E. G. Stanley Baker (Drew University)
John Baum (Oberlin College)
K. K. Clarke (Polytechnic Institute of Brooklyn)
Anthony Foderaro (The Pennsylvania State University)
Paul Foreman (The Pennsylvania State University)
Ira J. Gordon (University of Florida)
Jean Grambs (University of Maryland)
John W. Hamblen (Southern Regional Education Board)
Victor I. Howery (University of Wisconsin)
Kenneth Hunter (The Pennsylvania State University)
Clarence E. Jackson (Ohio State University)
Jacob Millman (Columbia University)
Lloyd M. Polentz (University of California)
J. D. Ryder (Michigan State University)
Amiya K. Sen (Columbia University)

William Shultz (City College of the City University of New York)
Kinsley R. Smith (The Pennsylvania State University)
Howard F. Stettler (University of Kansas)
William A. Sweeney (Choate School)
Kendall B. Taft (Roosevelt University)
George Thompson (Columbia University)
B. E. Tsagris (Arizona State University)
Kermit Waln (Thomas Jefferson High School, Denver)
E. T. Weiler (Purdue University)
Jay Young (Kings College)

Chapter Reviewers

Robert Allen (University of Miami)
C. R. Carpenter (The Pennsylvania State University)
Stephen M. Corey (University of Miami; formerly, Columbia University)
Robin Ferster (Academy La Castellana)
Joseph L. French (The Pennsylvania State University)
Neil F. Garvey (University of Illinois)
Cornelius W. Gillam (University of Pennsylvania)
Homer Kempfer (Director, U.S. Armed Forces Institute)
John M. Leslie (New York State Bureau of Private Trade and Correspondence Schools)
C. O. Neidt (Colorado State University)
William K. Selden (formerly, National Commission on Accrediting)
Ripley S. Sims (U. S. Armed Forces Institute)
Theresa Wilkins (U. S. Office of Education)
Ben M. Zeff (Office of the Assistant Secretary of Defense)

The special aid of the following is acknowledged with appreciation:

Jack Arbolino, Frank G. Dickey, Gale P. Gotschall, the late F. Lloyd Hansen, Otto Peters, Russell V. Ritchey, Alice Rowbotham,

J. D. Souder, Oscar F. Spencer, Israel Sweet, John Valley, and Martha Wallace.

Assisting the Research Staff during parts of the study:

Vera Adams, Margaret Bell, Eva Burke, John Christensen, Sara Close, Janice Dahlberg, Paul Dascher, Joy Foster, Shirley Guisewhite, Valerie Iwand, James Nace, Jean Serpa, Barbara Smith, Helen Smith, Judith Smith, and Alice Warne.

Index

Index